Clarence Jordan

Turning Dreams into Deeds

Clarence Leonard Jordan, 1912–1969

Clarence Jordan

Turning
dreams
into
deeds

by Henlee H. Barnette

ISBN 1-880837-00-5

Clarence Jordan. Turning Dreams into Deeds.
Copyright ©1992
Smyth & Helwys Publishing, Inc.
Printed in the United States of America

† † †

The paper used in this publication meets
the minimum requirements of American National Standard
for Information Sciences—Permanence of Paper
for Printed Library Materials, ANSI Z39.48-1984.

† † †

Library of Congress Cataloging-in-Publication Data

Barnette, Henlee H.
Clarence Jordan : turning dreams into deeds
/ by Henlee H. Barnette.
ix+108 pp.   5.25x8" (13.5x20.5 cm.)
ISBN 1-880837-00-5 : $9.95
1. Jordan, Clarence.   2. Koinonia Farm. I. Title.
BX6495.J65B37   1992
269'.2'092—dc20   92-9065
[B]   CIP

Contents

† **In memoriam** †

Clarence and Florence Jordan
Martin and Mabel England
cofounders of Koinonia Farm

and

Arthur and Nellie Steilberg
whose initial gift made Koinonia Farm possible

Preface

Now faith is the turning of dreams into deeds. . . .
—Hebrews 11:1, Cotton Patch Version

Koinonia Partners had its beginning in the heart and mind of Clarence Jordan. In 1942 he, his wife, and a missionary couple started the experiment near Americus, Georgia. It was called "Koinonia Farm." Its purpose was twofold: to build a racially inclusive community in which (1) Christians would live in radical obedience to Christ; and (2) those in fellowship would help local farmers, especially the poor.

During the 1950s Clarence's dream turned into a nightmare. He and his family were excommunicated from a Baptist Church. Members of the KKK sought to drive him out of Sumter County, Georgia. Koinonia Farm was boycotted, a roadside stand was bombed, and Clarence's home was riddled with bullets. Insurance was cancelled and merchants feared to do business with Koinonia Farm. By 1968 survival seemed to be in doubt.

Then Millard Fuller, a brilliant young businessman, entered the picture. Together, Millard and Clarence launched a new program and Koinonia Farm became Koinonia Partners. Today, the experiment continues to flourish.

Koinonia Farm occupies 1,500 acres, about 700 acres of which are for farming. A food processing industry is growing. Low-cost housing is available. There is a child development center. Koinonia has an impressive outreach program which provides paralegal assistance, counseling, care of foster children, and prison visitation.

A "fund for humanity" was established through which land could be bought and held in trust for families to farm in partnership. The fund also includes partnership in housing and industries. Surplus from farming, food products, and gifts go directly to the fund to meet human need. These monies support Koinonia industries to provide jobs and low-cost housing and rehabilitation. Also the Child Development Center and Youth Ministries share in these funds.

Clarence had concluded that

> What the poor need is not charity but capital, not caseworkers but coworkers. And what the rich need is a wise, honorable, and just way of divesting themselves of their overabundance.[1]

Koinonia Partners' has given birth to related organizations, most notably Habitat for Humanity in 1976. Habitat's purpose is to build housing for the poor. Thousands of such houses have been built in America and many foreign countries. Jubilee Partners was started in 1979 to aid refugee immigrants to North America. New Hope House opened in 1989 as a service to people who come to visit death row prisoners, providing meals, child care, and a place to rest.

The present volume is an expression of my reflections on Clarence Jordan and his prophetic vision and message, informed by my personal knowledge of him, his writings, lectures, sermons, and our many conversations. Also, relying on records of lectures and sermons, some of Clarence's own reflections and in his own words are presented. I also offer a selection of personal letters that reveal something more of the

---

[1]Dallas Lee, *The Cotton Patch Evidence* (New York: Harper & Row, 1971) 214-15.

inner man. Finally, a number of persons whose lives Clarence touched share some of their reflections on Clarence Jordan.

Chapter 1 is a portrait of the prophet, a collage of his character and action. Chapter 2 concerns Jordan's theological vision. Chapter 3 focuses some of his own thoughts on war and nonviolence. Chapter 4, on Koinonia Farm in transition, comprises selections from five lectures presented to the Christian Ethics classes at Southern Baptist Seminary as part of the Gheens Lectures in 1968.

The lectures are recorded as they were spoken in classes. Clarence's Southern drawl and dialect are clearly evident. This, coupled with his delightful sense of humor and radical Christian lifestyle, had a great impact upon students.

Appendix 1 consists of letters chosen form my correspondence with Clarence and his devoted wife Florence. In them one can gather insights into their personal feelings, struggles, hopes and dreams.

Appendix 2 includes reflections by some whose lives were enriched because they knew Clarence personally. Their comments reveal the radical commitment of Clarence to the Christian community in the midst of hostile social forces.

—Henlee H. Barnette

Clarence Jordan used this shack at Koinonia Farm as an office/study.
(Photograph by James M. Pitts.)

Chapter 1

The Prophet in Action

A prophet is one who speaks God's message with courage and without compromise. Our nation has produced a paucity of such prophets. But among the few authentic prophets are Abraham Lincoln, Walter Rauschenbusch, Georgia Harkness, Martin Luther King, Jr., and Clarence Leonard Jordan. Why do I classify these persons as prophets and God's speakers to their generations? Because they measure up to the characteristics of the biblical prophet.

1. Portrait of a Prophet

Biblical prophets are more *forth-tellers* than *fore-tellers* because they speak to current religious idolarty and social injustice. Prophets are grasped by a sense of divine vocation or calling; yet they are human, persons of finitude. Often, they suffer because they attack dehumanizing ideas and institutions both religious and secular that have become sacrosanct. Their lives may be threatened because they challenge powerful evil forces in high places. As Abraham Heschel observed, the prophets may be charged with "moral madness" because they do not fit in with the status quo of society.[1]

An authentic prophet is often lonely, "a voice crying in the wilderness." They do not cry, "Peace, peace," where there is no peace or purvey pious palaver to please and "tickle the ears" of their hearers.

---

[1]Abraham Heschel, *The Prophets* (New York: Harper & Row, 1962) ch.

They have a passion for justice and righteousness. Yet their stern demand for justice is tempered with mercy and love. Their ultimate goal or ideal is that of a redeemed people in a righteous community under the sovereignty of God.

After examining the lives and messages of Lincoln, Rauschenbusch, Harkness, King, and Jordan, I have come to the conclusion that they meet to a significant degree the above criteria of a genuine prophet of the God of revelation. For example, Lincoln's sencond inaugural address of March 4, 1865, is a profound theological and ethical prophetic statement. Almost everything Rauschenbusch wrote was prophetic, especially his *Christianity and the Social Crisis.* Harkness, a generation before the feminist movement, in her writings such as *Christian Ethics* (1957) spoke prophetically to the issues of racism, capitalism, war, and human rights. King's *Strength to Love* and *Trumpet of Conscience* contain prophetic elements. Jordan's *The Substance of Faith* is a collection of his earthy prophetic utterances in relation to social issues in the Deep South.

2. The Prophet's Challenge

Clarence Jordan has been called "a saint in overalls." He was that indeed, but also much more. He was a *prophet* in blue jeans—that is what he wore most of the time at Koinonia Farm, the interracial community he founded in 1942 near Americus, Georgia. Clarence always—like a true prophet—presented a powerful challenge to his hearers for action to meet human need.

My first encounter with Clarence was in 1941. He had recently received his Ph.D. from Southern Baptist Seminary and had come to speak in the seminary's small chapel, which was then in the north wing of Norton Hall. A tall, handsome, magnetic person with a gentle South Georgia drawl, he graphically described the deplorable situation in the ghettos of the city of Louisville. His portrayal of the famous (or infamous) Haymarket District intrigued me and the challenge he thrust upon us captivated me.

"If there is a student in this chapel who isn't looking for the First Baptist Church of Pondunk Hollow," he said, "there is a ministry for you in this city's Haymarket district where 10,000 people are unchurched." (Seminary professor Gaines Dobbins had surveyed the area and found that many unchurched.)

For several weeks Jordan's words kept surfacing in my mind, for my own pilgrimage had its roots in poverty and, later, in the hardening stress of the ghettos of the towns where I was a cotton mill laborer. In the milltown I had not sought out a church; rather, a caring fellow millhand had sought me out—with irritating persistence! Thus, on a rainy Saturday afternoon, a fellow seminary student and I decided to enter the Haymarket area to "see for ourselves" and perhaps to visit in some of the homes.

We went to an old tenement house near First and Jefferson Streets. The dingy stairs were foul smelling and rat infested. As we made our way up to the fourth floor, a flock of pigeons suddenly took flight from an opening in the stairwell. Now *there's* a sound to test one's commitment! Nevertheless, we continued our climb and found on that top floor a family of three living in two small rooms. Handmade bunk beds were built into the walls and the only source of heat was a two-burner kerosene stove. The father said they had been living there for twenty years and that we were the first ministers ever to visit their home.

During the next five years, I discovered in the Haymarket many other families who had never had a pastoral call, even for funerals. In September 1941, I became pastor of the old Union Gospel Mission in the midst of the Haymarket. It was part of the Long Run Baptist City Mission program directed by Clarence Jordan.

This Haymarket Community was unique in the 1940s. Before the advent of the auto and the supermarket, the Haymarket was the place where farmers brought and sold their produce in a semi-open place that covered a city block. The canopied sidewalks of Jefferson Street were still there in the early 1940s where other merchants hawked their wares from small stalls. Both wealthy and poor people purchased vegetables and fruits from this community.

The old mission house stood at First and Jefferson on the spot now occupied by a modern hotel. In the 1940s when I lived at the Mission, there were *ninety* whiskey stores, bars, "honky tonks," nightclubs, gambling dens, porno shops, and houses of prostitution all within a radius of three blocks.

I had planned to write my doctoral thesis about life in the Haymarket. Dr. Kutak, chairman of the Department of Sociology at the University of Louisville, helped me develop a research instrument. As any serious student is aware, every dissertation must have a sophisticated, scholarly sounding title. I came up with "A Critical Analysis of Commercial Recreation of an Urban Area in Transition." But, although I gathered the data, I never wrote that thesis. I was growing weary of limitations placed upon the program from denominational headquarters, of filling out detailed reports for the enhancement of reports to the association. I envisioned setting up a recreational facility for youth: a gymnasium and land with a lake in the country for camping. In short, a larger ministry. Also, I was struggling for a theology of such sordid slum conditions and, consequently, turned to Walter Rauschenbusch and Reinhold Niebuhr. My thesis centered on the ethical thought of Rauschenbusch who also had served a downtown Louisville church for two summers as an interim pastor while a seminarian, and later served a church on the edge of a slum called Hell's Kitchen in New York. Niebuhr was pastor of a church under the shadow of the Ford factories in Detroit with the concomitant economic and social problems.

Eventually, Louisville's Union Gospel Mission was given to the Long Run Baptist Association and, during the war years, became one of the largest missions of its kind in the Southern Baptist Convention. Most of the seminarians who worked with me at the mission, where I was later appointed superintendent, became well known in their chosen professions. Among these were Professors Henry Turlington, T. C. Smith, Jack Kilgore, Wayne Oates, and Victor Glass (a denominational executive), Carlyle Marney (a distinguished preacher and author), and John Walker (medical missionary to Africa).

3. The Prophet as Evangelist

During 1941 and 1942, Clarence, as superintendent of city missions for the Long Run Baptist Association, gave me a free hand to develop my own form of ministry. He was consistently there with his moral and spiritual support. He was present when I preached my first sermon at the mission September 7, 1941. Often he dropped in for prayer meeting or, when needed, he would teach a Sunday School class. Once he gave a voice recital for a club which met at the mission, and sometimes he would play his trumpet or sing at the morning worship service. His powerful singing of "The Holy City" was a favorite with the folks there.

From May 31 to June 11, 1942, Clarence served as evangelist for the annual spring revival at the mission. (I led the singing.) The first Monday night, there was a very small crowd, but Clarence preached as if thousands were present. Before the end of the week, nine had joined our mission by baptism and seven by letter. Some of these persons became devoted, solid leaders in the mission and in the community. Our evangelist refused an honorarium, but we gave him fifteen dolllars anyway, to help establish Koinonia Farm.[2] Soon Clarence would be leaving for—he thought at that time—Alabama to set up the farm. The site finally selected turned out to be in South Georgia—outside Americus, near a place called Plains.

4. The Prophet as Peacemaker

Before Clarence left Louisville, I recall the two of us were making footage of the Haymarket Community to be used in film presentations in local churches. We were across the street from Stony's Honky Tonk—which happened to be next to my residence. At Stony's during the past two years, there had been fifty-two publicized crimes—including two murders. (All this had been front-page news in

---

[2]Henlee Barnette, *Diary*, June 21, 1942.

The Courier Journal.) So when the owner spotted Clarence filming the front of his establishment, he rushed across Jefferson Street in a rage, bellowing curses, threatening to "beat hell" out of Clarence. As he prepared to do just that, Clarence, calm and unruffled, spoke in that soft, Southern drawl, "My friend, this *is* a free country, is it not?" This was hardly the response expected by the rough character who paused, nonplussed, then turned and retreated to Stony's with only an "Aw, to hell with you!" flung over his shoulder.

Bob Herndon who worked with Clarence in the black ghetto area of Louisville relates the following incident that occurred about 1939. A young black girl had been raped by a white man. Angry blacks met at the Negro Fellowship Center. A large black man leading the crowd waved a section of iron pipe saying, "Just like the whites kill a Negro for this, I'm going to kill a white man." When the man made this threat, Clarence (who had slipped into the meeting) stepped forward, laid his head on a nearby table and calmly said, "If a white man must die for this rape, let it be me. Do it now."

The enraged black man put down his weapon and the crowd murmured in astonishment. Some thoughtful discussion about action without violent recrimination followed this dramatic action.

5. The Prophet as Gracious Guest

After Clarence went to Georgia in 1942, we kept in touch by mail and an occasional visit several times from 1951 until his death. When he visited in our home, he was a refined and gracious guest who paid us the supreme courtesy of taking our children seriously. With those direct-yet-gentle eyes, he would give children his full attention and listen carefully to what they might share with him.

Clarence knew and practiced the art of being present where he was. He was intensely interested in each member of our family. You never felt that his mind was in some theological tome or back on the farm. He knew how to celebrate the present moment as if it were most meaningful. Our children remember Clarence as the man who gave them his full attention when he was our welcome guest.

6. The Prophet in Academia

Down on Koinonia Farm, Clarence felt the need for the intellectual stimulation of seminary and university. Once he wrote to me saying that "It would be good to sit down for a long chat with you. One of the most difficult things about being stuck off down here in Georgia is the lack of real stimulating, challenging conversation." On his visits to Louisville—his wife Florence was from Louisville and a daughter lived in Indiana—Clarence would come to my office at Southern Baptist Seminary and we would have long discussions about the growing edge of theological ethics.

Clarence met his need for intellectual stimulation by lecturing at seminaries and universities. On several occasions when he came to Louisville, I would have him lecture in my Christian Ethics classes. These lectures were not announced and he accepted no honoraria. I recall that, on one occasion, two students were so moved by this compelling speaker that they walked out of the class and left the seminary to return with Clarence to Koinonia Farm.

Edward McDowell, Jr., sometime professor of New Testament at Southern Seminary and a friend of Clarence, notes in his introduction to *The Cotton Patch Version of Hebrews and the General Epistles* that in 1968 Clarence was invited to speak at Southern Baptist Seminary. (Apparently, he had not been invited to speak in chapel, though he *had* been invited to lecture in ethics classes, since President Sampey invited him to in 1941.) McDowell notes, "Things do change."[3] Indeed, when I became chairman of the Special Lectureship Committee, I thought it was time to have Clarence lecture to the entire seminary community. His response to my invitation to give the Gheens Lectures reflected his reluctance to do this. His letter of May 15, 1968, read in part,

---

[3]Edward A. McDowell, Jr., "Introduction" to *The Cotton Patch Version of Hebrews and the General Epistles* by Clarence Jordan (New York: Association Press, 1973).

Those Gheens Lectures sound like mighty high cotton for a pea-picking farmer like me, and I'm sort of scared to tackle it. But at the same time, because of our personal friendship, I do not feel disposed to decline it.

Prior to this letter, Clarence had been lecturing at some of the most prestigious universities and seminaries in the country. His lectures at "Mother Seminary" had a significant appeal and impact. His chapel speech on "The Humanity of God" and his lectures in the Christian Ethics classes, including "Incarnational Evangelism" appear in his widely read volume *The Substance of Faith,* published posthumously.[4]

7. The Prophet as Interpreter

It was of supreme importance to Clarence that his deeds be grounded firmly in Scripture. I recall our quiet discussions of his views of the meaning of Acts 2:32 and his interpretation (see chapter 2, below). He never tried to coerce another person to accept his interpretation of Scripture. I leaned more toward W. O. Carver's view that the verb tenses in the Acts 2 and 4 passages indicated that the holding of all things in common by the disciples was not a once-and-for-all action, but rather an occasional action as need arose.[5] Dr. Carver had gone on to note that to surrender all of their goods once and for all would be to neglect the duty of responsible stewardship and to lose the discipline of administration.

While I could not accept completely Clarence's interpretation of the particular passages in Acts that provided the biblical basis for his communal endeavor, I believed in him, cherished his commitment and fortitude, and sought to be supportive of him and Koinonia Farm. There

---

[4]Clarence Jordan, *The Substance of Faith* (New York: Association Press, 1972).

[5]W. O. Carver, *The Acts of the Apostles*, The Convention Series (Nashville: Sunday School Board, Southern Baptist Convention, 1916) 52-59.

is a need for such models of radical economic sharing to shame us of our own greed and to motivate us to be more sharing with the needy.

8. The Prophet Rejected

Clarence was a prophet who had one foot in the Holy Scriptures and the other in an unholy society. He held that biblical teachings related to the conduct of life. He took Jesus seriously and, in addition, he read the Bible and attempted to practice what it says. This contributed to his alienation from politicians, some educational institutions, denominational bureaucrats, and church leaders.

An example Clarence related to me was a meeting he had, at his request, with the deacons of the small Baptist church near Koinonia Farm where he was a member. The church was threatening to excommunicate him. During the discussion, Clarence held up his Bible and implored, "Brethren, if I have violated any teaching of this book in my beliefs or conduct, I will withdraw quietly from this church fellowship. Please point to the text or teaching I have failed to try to live up to!" With that he handed the Bible to the deacon seated next to him who nervously passed it, unopened, to the next. This silent uneasy passing of the Book continued, until finally one deacon exploded, "Brother Jordan, don't pull that Bible stuff on us!"

"A prophet is not without honor save in his own country." So it was with Clarence in his own beloved Georgia where he was subjected to bombings, boycotts, and rejection. The church where he was a member excluded him, his family, and other Koinonia folk from membership. He felt that, generally, Southern Baptist denominational leaders did not wish to be identified too closely with him because of his views on race, religion, and economics. But, as often happens with prophets, this one in blue jeans is now—more than two decades following his death (in 1969)—receiving wider acclaim and adulation than he or anyone else ever expected. Dissertations have been written and are being written about him and Koinonia Farm; numerous books and articles about Clarence and his social experiment have been published for a wide readership; and a Broadway musical entitled *Cotton Patch Gospel* has received highly favorable reviews. This celebration of his views extended Clarence's influence into the secular arena in an unusual fashion.

Even some of his Baptist brethren are belatedly acknowledging him, now that he's been safely buried without a marker or monument in the red clay of Georgia. It has always been so: even some religious leaders praise dead prophets but cannot bear the living ones.

9. The Prophet Passes

Clarence kept a busy schedule right up to his death translating the New Testament (he was a superb Greek scholar), writing, lecturing, teaching God's word as he understood it. Indeed the day he died in that little isolated one-room shack which was his study out in the cornfield, he was preparing a lecture to be given the next day at Mercer University.

The local coroner refused to come to the farm and issue the death certificate. This prophet's body had to be driven into town in the back of a station wagon before the coroner would pronounce him dead. His body was buried the following afternoon wearing blue jeans in a homemade coffin as he had earlier requested. The funeral was simple, attended by many Clarence had ministered to, but no local church or community leaders attended other than one Baptist and one Presbyterian minister. After a brief service, some of the Farm people began covering the coffin with the dirt. A two-year-old girl, (Millard Fuller's daughter Faith) sensing that the moment required more than heavy silence, moved to the edge of the freshly dug grave and began to sing the only song she knew:

Happy Birthday to you;
Happy Birthday to you;

Happy Birthday, dear Clarence;
Happy Birthday to you![6]

I thank my God upon every remembrance of Clarence. Once I searched for his grave in that pine grove in Southwest Georgia. But, like the grave of the prophet Moses, there was no marker and I never found it. Yet, as I stood there and listened to the wind blowing gently through the pines, I felt his presence near. I could almost hear him say with a chuckle, "Henlee, Koinonia Partners is not the Kingdom of God on earth, but it's a lot closer to it than your capitalistic welfare state."

---

[6]Dallas Lee, *The Cotton Patch Evidence* (New York: Harper & Row, 1971); and Millard Fuller, *Bodotola* (New York: Association Press, 1977) 21-22.

Chapter 2

The Theological Vision
of the Prophet

Clarence Leonard Jordan, primary founder of Koinonia Farm near Americus, Georgia, was a farmer, preacher, author, Bible translator, lecturer, and theologian. He would not claim to be a theologian. Yet while he was not a systematic theologian, he was a biblical one. Jordan's theology grew out of his struggle with social injustice. From his encounter with injustice in society, he fashioned his theological stance.[1] The major ethical issues of Clarence's concern were war and peace, poverty, and racism.

Originally, Clarence was nurtured in the traditional theology of Southern Baptists. But as he encountered the moral issues of racial prejudice, the plight of the poor, the draft of World War II, he felt the need for a theological framework more adequate for his social passion and ethical concerns. This he had not found in either his church life or the seminary in Louisville. Both of these institutions were largely otherworldly oriented and promoted a privatized faith. James McClenden charges that the Bible teachers did not lead Jordan beyond his own conservative conception of the nature of the Bible and its ethical

---

[1]Cf. Walter Rauschenbusch's theological perspective, which grew out of his concern for economic justice; Reinhold Niebuhr's, from history and political science; Paul Tillich's, from ontology; Harvey Cox's and Gibson Winter's, from sociology.

demands.[2] But, while literary and form cirticism were not stressed by his professors, Clarence was introduced to the critical method in his advanced courses in New Testament. While he may not have gained much knowledge about ethical and social issues from his teachers, he learned a lot about Koine Greek. Once he told me, with a twinkle in his eye, that he learned a lot of New Testament Greek in spite of his teachers. He discovered in the Greek New Testament a scriptural basis for his moral passion and social action.

From Scripture and experience, Jordan developed his theological concepts of radical discipleship, koinonia, incarnational evangelism, and the God Movement or the Kingdom of God.

What I shall say about Jordan's theology and ethics is based primarily upon personal dialogues with him as a co-worker in the ghettoes of Louisville and across the years until his untimely death, his sermons in the Haymarket Mission where I was co-laborer with him, lectures in Christian Ethics classes during his occasional visits to Louisville's Southern Seminary and the Gheens Lectures of 1968 there. From publications, the most adequate expression of Clarence's theological ethics is in his work, *The Substance of Faith*, published posthumously.[3] Some of the messages of this volume were given in the Christian Ethics classes at Southern Baptist Seminary. James McClenden, Jr. *Biography as Theology* presents the most serious analysis of Clarence's theological ideas.[4]

---

[2]James McClendon, *Biography as Theology* (Nashville: Abingdon Press, 1974) 117.

[3]Clarence Jordan, *The Substance of Faith* (New York: Association Press, 1972).

[4]McClendon, *Biography as Theology*, chap. 5.

1. Radical Discipleship

To be a follower of Christ, Clarence believed, involved total commitment to His will and way. The first step in this direction involves repentance. Clarence deplored the ambiguity of the term repentance for the Greek word *metanoia*. Repentance for him was more than feeling sorry about getting caught at something wrong. Rather it is more like a metamorphosis, meaning to change form, like the caterpillar that changes into a butterfly. It results in a complete transformation of life.[5] This is what it means to be "born from above."

Another spiritual fact essential to radical Christian discipleship is faith in God through Christ. Faith is basic to Jordan's theological vision. He translates Hebrews 11:1 as follows: "Now faith is the turning of your dreams into deeds; it is betting your life on the unseen realities."[6] Faith is not mere belief in spite of a lack of evidence, but a life in spite of consequences.[7] One of the basic weaknesses of liberalism, Jordan thought, is that it accepts the life of Jesus, but shuns the inevitable consequences, namely, the crucifixion.

For Jordan, faith or belief in Christ means more than intellectual assent to a Christological proposition. Rather, faith is trustful obedience to God, the translation of conviction into conduct.

Clarence was aware that the church was and is often captive to culture. He insisted that one must ultimately choose between Christ and the cultural traditions of the age. After having preached in a Southern church, Clarence observed an elderly woman

> as crisp with pride as a dead honeysuckle vine making her way down the aisle, her eyes telegraphing the tone of her response to his message. He braced, and she delivered—straight from the

---

[5]Jordan, *The Substance of Faith*, 94-97.

[6]Clarence Jordan, *The Cotton Patch Version of Hebrews and the General Epistles* (New York: Association Press, 1973).

[7]Jordan, *The Substance of Faith*, 42.

gut level of her culture, "I want you to know that my grandfather fought in the Civil War, and I will never believe a word you say."

Clarence who was tall and gracious and Southern as sowbelly himself, smiled and replied, "Ma'am, your choice seems quite clear. It is whether you will follow your granddaddy or Jesus Christ."[8]

Faith, for Clarence, was a basic element in radical discipleship. Faith is existential and means participating in God's action in the world. A key to Clarence's theological ethics is found in Paul: "Faith active in love" (Gal 5:6, NEB).

A keen student of words, Clarence further illuminates his idea of faith by examining the etymology of *belief*. Our English term *belief* stems from the old Anglo-Saxon *be* which means "by" and *lief* which means "life." Hence, what one lives by is one's belief or "bylife." So, faith and life are inseparable. It is the "activation of our aspirations, convictions translated into deeds."[9] Fear is the thing that makes it difficult to have faith. "Fear is the polio of the soul," Clarence observes, "which prevents our walking by faith."[10]

Radical discipleship—that is, discipleship with roots—means that we may have to, in the words of Luther, "let goods and kindred go." Clarence relates how when things were going against Koinonia Farm, he approached his brother, a lawyer, to represent Koinonia Farm in legal matters. (His brother later became a state senator and chief justice of the Georgia Supreme Court.) Because of his political aspirations, the brother declined. Clarence reminded him that when they both joined the church, the preacher asked them the same question: "Do you accept Jesus as Savior and Lord?" Clarence said to his brother: "I answered 'Yes!' What did you say?" His brother responded: "Clarence, I follow Jesus up to a point." "Could that point," asked Clarence, "be to the cross?"

---

[8]Ibid., introduction.
[9]Ibid., 43.
[10]Ibid.

"That's right," said his brother, "I follow Him to the cross, but not on the cross. I'm not going to get myself crucified." "Then I don't believe that you are a disciple," responded Clarence. "You are an admirer of Jesus but not a disciple." Today his brother is a believer and is proud, as he says, to be the brother of "the greatest Christian I have ever known."

Clarence always spoke candidly and unambiguoulsy about being a Christian. He was easily understood. He never camouflaged his message in pious platitudes or the latest political or "religious bureaucratese from headquarters." He was scriptural in his speech, for his *yea* was *yea* and *nay* was *nay*. As with Jesus, this often got him into trouble with the religious, economic, and social status quo.

2. Koinonia

Pursuing his studies at Southern Baptist Seminary in the Greek New Testament, Clarence discovered in the book of the Acts of the Apostles both a model and a means of expressing his concern for a truly Christian community. In Acts is recorded the episode of a spontaneous brotherhood of radical sharing of goods in the primitive church. Acts 2:44-45 reads: "And all that believed were together, and had all things common [*koina*]; and they sold their possessions and goods, and parted them to all, according as any man had need" (ASV). A similar passage in Acts 4:32 reads: "And the multitude of them that believed were of one heart and soul: and not one of them said that aught of the things which he possessed was his own; but they all had things common [*koina*]" (ASV).

Clarence interpreted these passages to mean more than the current popular concept of "fellowship" in the churches in terms of meeting, eating, and then retreating to the comforts of homes. Rather he held that *koinonia* called for radical sharing of goods, worship, and witness.

To implement his dream, Clarence attempted to find a Koinonia or a fellowship of radical economic sharing composed of seminarians at Southern Baptist Seminary. Participiants, about a dozen, pooled their resources. Each received cash when in need of food, clothing, and other essentials. One of the leading couples who put in $100.00 withdrew it and left the movement because they were expecting a baby and the group declined to authorize a special type of medical therapy which the couple felt was needed. The group felt that the medical treatment sought was too expensive and really not needed.

Clarence urged members of the new social experiment to worship in black churches in the city. He set the example by joining a black Baptist church. Many of the group attended black churches where they worshiped and served in various roles. Some students served in the Union Gospel Mission and Baptist Fellowship Center. The latter was a mission for blacks, offering worship, recreation, and counseling for the poor in the Westend of Louisville.

Some students in the group worked at The Union Gospel Mission in the Haymarket district of Louisville because they wanted to spend the summer there after the school term ended. Arrangements were made and the students agreed to share their meager possessions. So during the summer these students lived in a form of koinonia.

For the members of this "Koinonia," Clarence provided a study group on the seminary campus. During their study sessions, Clarence shared his views on pacifism, racism, and radical economic sharing in a common life.

In downtown Louisville, Clarence opened the Lord's Store House. Here people and churches could contribute used goods such as clothing, furniture, canned goods, and other items. These goods were sold to the poor for low prices or given to those who could not pay. Members of Koinonia helped to operate this project.

These social experiments grew out of Clarence's vision of a Christian community in its embryonic stage. These early experiments failed due to the fact that the group did not really live together, work together, worship together, study together, and pray together. Furthermore, students in transition did not lend stability to the group: at graduation they went their separate ways. It was wartime and some went to work in defense plants. One of the group even enlisted in the Army and rose to the rank of colonel.

Clarence realized that to succeed his experiment needed an agricultural setting where members could live, worship, work, and share together in a more or less independent and interdependent community. In 1942, he and his wife Florence, along with Martin England and his wife Mable (former missionaries to India) settled on 400 acres of rundown farmland near Americus in southwest Georgia. Here Koinonia Farm became a reality. Twenty-six years later, in 1968, Millard Fuller, a young lawyer and millionaire, gave his money away, joined the Koinonia fellowship, and with Clarence founded Koinonia Partners and the Fund for Humanity.

The history and present status of the Koinonia experiment would make an exciting doctoral dissertation. At present, Dallas Lee's *The Cotton Patch Evidence* is the most comprehensive published treatment of the subject. Suffice it to say that today Koinonia Partners is alive and well. It is one of the most successful intentional communal experiments in living in the South. The basic principles upon which it is based are: total commitment to Christ; distribution according to need; no favorite children in the family; and "practicing the truth in love."

In a Christian Ethics class at Southern Baptist Seminary during 1968, Clarence described in detail the transition from Koinonia Farm to Koinonia Partners.[11] A couple of years earlier, he began to think about making some changes at Koinonia. Then Clarence, with the help of Millard Fuller, reorganized Koinonia. It has been thriving ever since under the name of Koinonia Partners.

In Sumter County and all over Georgia, farmers were losing their property to big insurance companies, especially to John Hancock of Hartford, Connecticut. Whites were moving to towns in the South and many blacks to Hartford to get jobs or to get on welfare. The cost to Hartford was astrononmical. Clarence declared that he would keep each black about to migrate to Hartford on a farm for $50,000—a real bargain in comparison to what the migrant would cost Hartford if he or she

---

[11]Gheens Lectures at Southern Baptist Theological Seminary, October 2, 1968, tape recording.

moved there. If his offer ever reached Hartford, it was not accepted.

The dream of Partners' Plan was to purchase a million acres of land from donations. This would be held in a nonprofit "Fund for Humanity" which would lend the land to the poor in terms of farms without interest. Clarence believed those who profited by the use of the land would voluntarily contribute to the Fund for Humanity so others could "borrow" land and farm it. Family allowances were to go to those in the Partnerships. It all began to work! Unfortunately, Clarence died within a year of the launching of Koinonia Partners.

3. Incarnational Evangelism

There is really only one "method" of evangelism in the New Testament: the incarnation of God in Jesus Christ. God made His good news, the "Idea"—Clarence translates *Logos* or "Word" as "Idea"—known to mankind by becoming a man. In Jesus, God became visible. While Jesus is truly the divine Son of God, the opposite side of his deity is the humanity of God. We have stressed the deity of Jesus to the exclusion of his humanity. We deify Jesus and deny his humanity in order to relieve ourselves from the awesome responsibilities we have to face if we affirm his humanity. We substitute liturgy for service, praise for the power to act, emphasis on buildings and budgets for ministry to the homeless and the poor.

People have ears to hear but they don't hear. But they can usually see. When Clarence first went to South Georgia, he preached in churches and expected to be in big trouble. But the deacons came by and complimented him on his "sweet sermon." However, as Koinonia took shape and the "word became flesh" and they could *see* it, a racially integrated community, they caught on. He was never asked to preach in those churches anymore.

New Testament evangelism then is to confront people with the visible Word. Clarence describes the current fate of incarnation as

> The word became a sermon and was later expanded into a book
> and the book sold well and inspired other books until of the

making of books there was no end. And the world died in darkness and was buried in the theological library.[12]

Incarnational evangelism is not only visible but total. It embraces the whole person. Clarence once preached a remarkably original sermon on the Gadarene demoniac (Luke 8:26-39) to illustrate this point. Here evangelism tackles one of the worst socioeconomic problems and one of the worst spiritual problems. Jesus' evangelism healed the man of his intrapsychic conflicts and eliminated what produced the man's despair. But that was not all. This kind of evangelism surrounded him with a fellowship and dressed him with some of their clothes, and then sent him back home to be a witness of God's grace in his own community.[13]

4. The Church

For Clarence, both the church and koinonia are continuations of the incarnation of the life, death, and resurrection of Jesus. For Clarence, the church is to be "the womb of God." Just as Mary was pregnant with Jesus, the Son of God, so the church in a real sense is to "give birth" to children of God, for the church is the womb in which they are conceived. Mary is replaced by the church. But the mother instinct in Mary caused her to want to keep Jesus as *her* son; she realizes, however, that she can keep him only by surrendering him as God's gift to mankind.

According to Clarence, the early church was willing to become pregnant. But he asserts that the contemporary church, God's bride, appears to have passed menopause, has gotten on the pill, or has gone a-whoring. When the church does the latter and becomes pregnant and bears children, they are not in the image of God.

Before Clarence had finished his seminary courses, he had come to feel that churches generally had been captured by culture, had become enclaves of racism, and were concerned with petty programs of self-enhancement. He challenged these issues in the church of which he was

---

[12]Jordan, *The Substance of Faith,* 33.
[13]Ibid., 36-37.

a member. In August 1950, he was excommunicated form the Rehoboth
Baptist Church near Koinonia Farm. Indeed, the entire Koinonia family
was excluded. The stated reason was that Koinonians' "views and
practices" were "contrary to those of other members of Rehoboth
Church." Such practices included visiting black churches and holding
worship services "where both white and colored attend together."[14] The
Jordans were not welcome in other churches in the community. So they
never again tried to join a church. When asked about his denominational
affiliation, Clarence, with a twinkle in his eye, would reply, "Ex-
Baptist."

5. The God Movement

Clarence's ethical ideal was that of a community in which the love
of God, personal equality, and economic justice could find full
expression by its members regardless of race, class, or nationality. He
sought an all-embracing theological concept that would support his ideal.
He discovered it in the doctrine of the Kingdom of God. Generally,
Clarence translates *baseleia* as "the God Movement." He also renders
it "New Order," "Spiritual Order," "Kingdom Movement," "Spiritual
Movement," and "Spiritual Family."

As a movement, the Kingdom of God involves spontaneity and
submission. It is a movement that happens and one must join it, receive
it, enter it, inherit it. But Clarence saw no contradiction between his
activism and the Kingdom as a movement. To be in the "God
Movement" was to incarnate in one's life the ethics of the Kingdom:
the ethics of love, justice, and compassion. But these principles are
abstractions until they become flesh, visible in the service of one's
neighbor. The ethical content of the Kingdom is clearly seen in the
Sermon on the Mount.

According to Clarence, Jesus constantly sought to concretize the

---

[14]Dallas Lee, *The Cotton Patch Evidence* (New York: Association Press,
1972) 77-78.

God Movement. According to some translations Jesus said to the Pharisees, "The kingdom of God is within you" (Luke 17:21). But Clarence held that Jesus did not use the term "within" (Luke 17:21). By *entos humon*, Jesus meant "in your midst" or "among you." The Kingdom could not have been *in* the Pharisees because they were being confronted by it.[15]

To be a member of the God Movement is to expect persecution at times. Persecution is the lot of those who take Jesus and His teachings seriously. Contrary to the popular "show biz" preachers who claim that contributing to their programs brings instant affluence in return, folks who practice unlimited love in this world may end up on a cross.

The God Movement confronts the Kingdom of Evil provoking scorn and suffering. No one understood this better than Clarence. Yet he was out to change his world. For him, to change the world was more than a slogan. He was aware that slogans, especially religious ones, are generally irrelevant and harmless unless acted out. So he tried to change a small section of South Georgia. His reward was that he and his fellow Koinonians were victims of persecution, bombing, economic boycott, and ostracism. He and his family were threatened with death, and on occasion bullets missed them by inches. In addition, Clarence was branded a communist by some who disagreed with him. But Clarence thought that a Christian was not earning his salt if he or she had never been labeled a communist. He never wavered in his belief that he was doing God's will and work. He was perfectly aware of the fact that without the shedding of blood, there is no radical social change in the world. He courageously challenged evil in society, paid the price, and emerged a winner.

We have briefly examined the theological vision of Clarence Jordan. We may not agree with some of his theology or his economic philosophy, but we cannot help but admire the man.

---

[15]Jordan, *The Substance of Faith*, 61.

On an ancient church in Europe are two sculptured groups: St. Martin cutting his cloak in two parts with his sword to clothe a beggar, and St. George spurring his horse against the dragon that devastated the country. Clarence was a man who embodied both kinds of sainthood in one life. His lifestyle of compassion for the poor and defenseless, and his courage in the face of evil, provides a model for us all.

Chapter 3

The Christian,
War, Violence, and Nonviolence

[This lecture was one of five that Clarence Jordan delivered at the Southern Baptist Theological Seminary as the Gheens Lectures, October 1962. This lecture (and the one that appears below in chapter 4) is transcribed from a tape recording.]

* * *

Since many questions have been raised about the Christian and war, the Christian and violence, nonviolence, and so forth, I thought perhaps that tonight I would just kind of share with you some of the experiences which we have had in this whole area ourselves. Now, to begin with, Koinonia committed itself to the idea of nonviolence, and it was rooted in the theological concept that God is love, and that the basis of this is the Golden Rule. So, in 1942, when Koinonia was begun, we boldly asserted that—even to a nation at war—that this was out of keeping with the Christian teaching.

Now when I went to register for the draft (in 1938, I believe it was, or 1939, whenever the first draft was), I wanted to register as a conscientious objector and tried to, but the draft board classified me as 4-D. Now I don't know whether they still have those same classifications or not, but that was the classification, when I looked it up, for prisoners, the feebleminded, and preachers. While I did not object to my fellow classes, I did not want to be in a specially exempt class. I felt that I wanted to make my protest and that I should not be exempt as a minister. Now I think one of the worst things, one of the most immoral things that we do, is to continue to accept the ministerial deferment. I think we ought to stand on our own two feet and say, "Classify me like you would a deacon, or an elder, or anybody else in the church." And I tried to fight that through. I went to the draft board and every way that I knew and, finally, they said, "Well, as long as you are an ordained minister, we got our rules and regulations to go by and we are going to classify you in 4-D." So they left me in that, and that was when we decided to set up our own little alternative to war and start Koinonia Farm.

Now in that was deeply rooted this idea of Christian pacifism, if you want to call it that. I don't call it that, but this is the idea. Now, we did not realize when we started Koinonia and committed ourselves to nonviolence and love that we would be given so many opportunities to practice it. But, time moved along and people began to find out what we were talking about, and that's always a very dangerous thing to do. I think the worst thing that Jesus ever did was to preach so people could understand him. When you start preaching that way, you get into a lot of difficulties.

Now the earliest opposition that came to Koinonia was not over our race views. The Southern people at that time thought they had at least another century to think over this race problem. We contained it pretty well. We were going to think it over, so they could admit a few crackpots here and there who violated the Southern code. Now, later on the Supreme Court came in with its decision that the schools had to be desegregated, and we had to proceed with all deliberate speed. You start talking to a man in Southwest Georgia about speed on anything and you're going to get him kind of upset. We move kind of slow there as you fellow Georgians know. I talk slow, I think slow, I even sleep slow. And the Supreme Court told us we had to move fast. Well, that in itself was enough to get a Southerner aroused, and that we had to move in this other area.

Now it was not until 1956 that the race thing began to horn in on us and that we had many, many opportunities to practice this whole business of nonviolence. But, in the earlier days, the opposition to us centered around this view on nonviolence. Now, if some of you who are on the faculty will forgive one little story I told last night. . . .

We had hardly been there just a few days when an old farmer came down there and he was all upset. He said, "I . . . I . . . I want to tell you . . . tell you something. You know what I don't like about you . . . you folks?"

I could have given quite a catalog of things but I said, "What?"

He said, "I don't like it 'cause you won't fight."

I said, "Who told you we wouldn't fight?"

He said, "That's what they're telling around here. You won't fight."

I said, "Well, you got us wrong, Mister. We'll fight."

"Will you fight?"

"Yes, sir," I said, "we'll fight."

He said, "How come you ain't at the war if you'll fight?"

I said, "Well, we don't fight with those kinds of weapons."

He said, "How do you fight?"

"Well," I said, "we fight with love, and justice, and truth, and mercy, and prayer, and patience, and forbearance."

And I saw I was losing him. Any time you start talking to a South Georgia farmer and ask questions, you're going to lose him. So I had to get a little bit more concrete.

Well, I happened to see one of our mules with his head stuck out of the barn down there and a big old ear flopped over and a long old face—looked like this farmer! So I said, "You see that old mule?"

"Yeah, I see him."

I said, "If you happen to walk down there by that old barn and that old mule reached out and bit you in the seat of the britches, would you bite back?"

"No, I wouldn't bite that mule back."

I said, "Well, why not?"

"'Cause I ain't no mule."

I said, "All right, I'll take your word for it. You're no mule." And I said, "What would you do?"

He said, "I'd get me a two-by-four and I'd beat his brains out."

"Oh, in other words, you wouldn't let the mule choose the weapon? If he wants to bite, you ain't going to bite, huh? You're going to get a weapon that the mule can't use and you'll beat its brains out."

"Yeah," he said, "that's what I'd do."

I said, "That's the way it is with us, too. It isn't that we won't fight. We just don't fight on the devil's level. We don't let him choose the weapon. You go to a jungle and want to fight with a lion, you going to let the lion choose the weapon? No! He chooses tooth and fang or fang and claw. You choose fang and claw and that lion will beat you. You better not let *him* choose the weapon. *You* better choose the weapon. So it is with us Christians. *We* choose the weapon. We do not let the devil choose our means of fighting."

Well, I don't think we convinced him, but later on, more and more violence arose growing out of this racial thing. At first it was a kind of nonviolent violence. You know, it's strange that during the time that the Negroes were fighting with nonviolence in Montgomery the white folks were fighting with nonviolence on the other side of the fence over in South Georgia against us. In fact, they clearly stated that we learned something from those Negro people, that they got a pretty good trick up their sleeve, and so they decided to fight us with boycotts. And this was the most difficult means of repelling, in which they just absolutely refused to buy or sell anything to us. But then that set the stage for this more violent approach, and this is the point that I want to come to tonight.

After the economic pressure failed to get us out, then came about a long-sustained program of violence and this really tore at our hearts because we had committed ourselves to active good will, that we would not fight back under any circumstances. And, in a very short while, we were being besieged with guns. One night, a car came by with a machine gun mounted on it just raking the community with tracer bullets, six and eight bullets going through the room at a time, just strafing the whole community, and that caused us to really reexamine our whole position of nonviolence. How far do you take this thing? These bullets narrowly missed our children. Do you stand aside? Do you not even buy a gun? Do you do nothing to protect your children?

Then on another occasion, my oldest daughter was home from college for spring vacation. She and I were sitting in the living room talking about 10:30 one night. She said, "Well, Dad, I'm a little bit tired. I think I'll go to bed." She got up and went to her bedroom, and I got up from my chair and started into our bedroom. Just about that moment, I heard the crack of rifles and bullets started ripping through the house. She had gone over to the window to pull down the shades and, when she did, she was silhouetted against the light and a high-powered deer rifle cracked out and the bullet ripped in beside her right at the window. That came through the wooden frame building, came ripping in just about a foot to the side of her, went through that wall on past her, hit the mirror hanging over her dresser on the wall and shattered that, went through that wall on into the living room where we were just sitting. And later, I sat back down in that chair and I could trace the path of that bullet right on out. (It would have gone right through my head if I had not gotten up just a few seconds earlier.) It went on through the living room through the door, into my wife's and my bedroom, went across that room into the wall, smashed through that into the closet of the children's room, yet through a box of jigsaw puzzles, went through another box of tinker toys, and finally came to rest in a tote that was hanging on the closet.

Well, a little later on, the sheriff came out to investigate it and came to the conclusion that it was not a BB gun and it was at that time that I felt myself filled with great anger and I really questioned whether this whole business was worth it or not. Here it came within just a very fraction of killing my daughter. And I was really amazed at the anger that flooded me and the desire for revenge that came over me. Now, while I was at the University of Georgia, I took advanced military and one of the things I got was two or three medals for expert marksmanship with the rifle. Now these law enforcement officers claimed that they had been unable to get any evidence. I thought if I could get an old rifle and lay down in a gully—a ditch—out there by our place, very shortly I'd be able to get the sheriff some evidence; some *warm* evidence. And I must confess that this desire almost posessed me. That's when I could just hardly resist giving up and going out and getting into this kind of response.

On another night, I remember I heard a terrific explosion. We had a roadside market over about four or five miles from our place located on the main U.S. highway north and south and we were selling country products—country ham and vegetables, eggs, and so forth. And five miles away, I could hear the explosion. A few minutes later the phone rang and somebody said, "You'd better get over here, your market has been blown up." We had just built that little old place the year before. I built it with my own hands. Many of the marks on the wall were blood marks where I had busted my finger and used a lot of my Hebrew. And, I mean, when you sweat for something like that, you get a sense of proprietorship in it—of ownership—and, as Harry Atkinson and I went over this little old store, I had once again this feeling that that was our place. Those so-and-so's had destroyed our property! And I remember, as we came over the rise and it was burning and we could see the glow on the horizon, the flow of anger and the desire for revenge that was within my heart at that time. So I have not been able in all of these years to keep from thinking evil thoughts and feeling anger and hate almost posessing me.

On another occasion, I was with my wife before they blew up this little roadside market. My wife and I were keeping it open and we'd go back and forth from the farm every day. And every morning at 8:00 we'd get in this little old car and we'd drive over this country road four or five miles to this little market and every afternoon at 5:00, we'd close it up and drive back over this same little road. There was a narrow, one-way bridge and narrowed out a little bit. Trees were hanging all over the place, and I said to my wife, "You know, honey, we ought not to be traveling this route so predictably. Our schedule is too regular. We ought not to come at the same time and we ought to vary the routes we could take." There were four or five routes that we could have taken to get over there. Just about that time, we came around a curve and headed down toward that one-way bridge. Well, I saw a pickup truck parked right to the right of it and, when we came around this curve, this truck moved over and got right into the bridge and stopped. Well, I had become rather suspicious and I had slowed down and had just about come to a stop myself when I saw a guy get out with a shotgun. Well, I remembered what Jesus said: if a man smites you on the right cheek, turn to him both heels. And I put that thing in reverse and got out of there. Now I didn't think that I'd be doing him a favor to let him murder me. I didn't want a man to have that on his conscience and love, in that case, demanded that I just get the so-and-so out of there *real quick*! And that's what I did. Now whether or not he shot, I don't know, because that thing was going at supersonic speed in reverse when we finally backed out of there and we went home another route.

Now I could go on and on and on illustrating time and time again why this thing is challenging. I think the point at which I came closest to giving it up was about three years ago, I believe. My little daughter was in high school. We'd had to take the school board to court to make them let her in—a white kid to a white school. We had to take them before the federal judge, get an injunction, and make them let our kids come to school. So she was there by court order and I said to her, "Now, Jan, honey, we won the case in the court, but there isn't a court in all the land that can make these folks love you. Now, they are going to be unkind and I'm just wondering if you really want to go to school here. If you don't, well, we'll send you somewhere else. We don't want you to feel that you are a victim of circumstances."

She said, "Daddy, I want to go to school here. I think we got some ideas that these folks need to hear."

I said, "Okay, Jan, you go to school here."

Well, she made it the first year and she made it the second year. She went through four years of high school there and not *once* in all of those four years did *any one* kid say "Good morning" to her. *Nobody* ever greeted her. At no time did any kid sit beside her in the school cafeteria.

If she was sitting at a table where some of the others were—if she sat down with them—they'd all take their trays and move away. If she was sitting alone, sometimes they'd walk around, she said, ten to fifteen minutes waiting for her to get up so they could sit down rather than sit at the table with her. They were big tables and she'd be there alone. She told me one day, she said, "You know, Daddy, I've learned to eat real slow."

For four years this kept up, but her last year was a real test, I think, both for her and for me. She said to me along in the spring, she said, "Dad, I don't know whether I can make it or not."

"What's your trouble, Jan?"

She said, "This little boy, Bob Speck, he's just about to drive me crazy."

She said, "For all the year now, every time I go from my home room down the hall to some other room, this little old boy meets me and he starts calling me all kinds of foul names—communist, whore, and all that kind of stuff—just as loud as he can, and then he just laughs as though he had thought up something original. He does that four or five times a day, and he's been doing it every day during the week since school started." (And this was in the spring.)

And I said, "Jan, you just don't have to take that kind of stuff. I'll go and talk to his mama and daddy."

She said, "Would you really?"

I said, "Yeah, I will."

She said, "I wish you luck."

I said, "What do you mean?"

She said, "His mama and daddy are members of the Ku Klux Klan and probably trained him in this exercise."

Well, I didn't go to talk to his mama and daddy, but I said, "I'm going to talk to that school principal."

She said, "And I wish you luck."

I said, "Well, I'm going."

And I went. And I talked to the man. I said, "Look, fella, my little girl has been taking this for three years and going into four years. These kids abuse her, push her down the stairs, all that kind of stuff, tear her books up, go in her desk, all that kind of stuff. I think she's had enough and I believe you can stop it."

"Oh, Mr. Jordan, that's just the way with high school kids. They just call one another names. They're perfectly normal."

And I could get nowhere with that man. So, finally, I went home and said, "Jan, I haven't gotten anywhere, but I tell you what I'm gonna do. I'm going to come to school this afternoon. As soon as school's out, I want you to come out on the school grounds and meet me. And then I want you to point out to me Bob Speck. I've tried to be a follower of Jesus and he taught me to love my enemies and all like that, but at that time, I'm going to ask Jesus to excuse me for about fifteen minutes while I beat the hell out of Bob Speck."

That little gal looked me in the eye and she said, "Daddy, you can't be excused from being a Christian for fifteen minutes."

I said, "Well honey, I guess you're right. I've made too many affirmations of my faith in the Lord Jesus. I don't suppose he would excuse me. I'm an old dyed-in-the-wool Christian, but you know, you're young and you haven't made the affirmations that I have, and I tell you what I want you to do. I want you to let your fingernails grow about three inches, and then I want you to get all the books you got in your arms, and I want you to walk down the hall. And when Bob Speck calls you those names, I want you to throw the whole bunch of books in his face and jump on him and scratch his eyes out, because I think for a kid to be scratched up by a girl would be a good lesson for him."

She said, "Daddy, you're not serious."

I was. I didn't know what else to do. I said, "Well, I . . . I don't know; I don't know whether I can be Christian under this circumstance any longer. If you won't beat him up, it looks like I'm gonna have to beat him up."

She said, "No, you're not going to beat him up."

Well, about, oh, two or three weeks passed and she said nothing more about it. So I brought up the subject. I said, "Jan, what are we going to do about Bob Speck?"

She said, "Who?"

I said, "Bob Speck."

She said, "Bob Speck? Oh, yeah, yeah. He doesn't bother me any more."

"Oh, he doesn't? Has he moved?"

"No, he's still there."

"Oh, has he been converted?"

"No," she said, "he hasn't been converted."

"Does he ever call you any names?"

"No, he never calls me any names."

I said, "What in the world has happened to him?"

"Well," she said, "I got to figuring out that I'm a little taller than Bob and I could see him before he could see me. When I'd see him, I'd begin smiling and waving and gushing at him like I was just head over heels in love with him. 'Hi, Bob! Hi!' I'd just go all the way down the hall just looking like I was going to eat him up! The other kids got to teasing him about me having a crush on him and, now, the only time I see him is when he peeps around the corner to see if I'm coming. If I am, he goes all the way round the outside. He doesn't bother me any more."

Well, young kids maybe can think of creative ways of dealing with evil that an older Christian can't. And I think this is what we got to do. This old slug-them-beat-them-up-and-destroy-them idea is just so uncreative. There's nothing new about that. It's something we've been trying for many hundreds of years, and it hasn't worked. But we don't know anything else to do, so we just go through the same old motions. Maybe we need to turn loose our kids with some creativity in this thing, to find new ways and new methods of dealing with evil. So, as I talk to you, I am not trying to say that I have been creative enough, but I think our kids have done a marvelous job with this. I remember on one occasion as the school bus came towards Koinonia, the other kids would laugh at the Koinonia kids and kinda hold their noses, and our kids took it in great stride. I said, "What did you do?"

They said, "Oh, we just told the kids they didn't have to hold their noses, they wouldn't come off."

You know, just that kind of dealing with a situation with good humor, good will, and laughing it off. I think there is something creative about this and I think there is something creative about Jesus when he said if a man slaps you on the right cheek, let him have the other and smile at him. If he makes you go a mile, go two. There is something creative, there is something redemptive about that. We ought to catch the imagination of it all. I am sure there are many other ways than just turning the right cheek. I think I mentioned a moment ago turning both heels. I think that is wonderfully creative. Let's get out of there. I've had to do that many a time. I think there is something creative about letting a man see your heels.

I remember I was brought up before the grand jury down there in Sumter County. They were investigating us because they said we were doing all the shooting, bombing, and blowing up of our place, and burning it up. And I spent two days before the grand jury. The foreman of the grand jury was questioning me. He said, "Mr. Jordan, I want to ask you a straightforward question, and I want you to give me a straightforward answer and answer me Yes or No."

I said, "Well, now. Mr. Bartlett, that could be a matter of semantics."

"Didn't ask if you were a semantic, I asked you if you were a Communist."

I said, "Well now, we just got to communicate, make sure that these words mean the same thing."

So I started in trying to distinguish between Karl Marx and Jesus. I began by asking him this way: I said, "You've asked me that question, now maybe I could ask you one. You've read about the Apostle Paul, I suppose?"

Nobody gave any affirmation sign, so I said, "Well, perhaps surely you have read the Communist manifesto."

And great silence prevailed.

"Well, gentlemen, surely you have read the constitution of the U.S.S.R?"

No sign that it had been read. And I saw right then that trying to distinguish between the teachings of Marx and the teachings of Jesus to people who knew nothing about either was a hopeless proposition. So I quit to change the subject.

This guy came back and he raised the question with me on this nonviolence thing. He knew how I was feeling about that. He said, "You know what the two foundations of the . . . " he started. He cussed and said, "Now, wait a minute! I'm a son of a . . . son of a . . . ," and I thought he was going to tell the truth, but he said, "I'm the son of a Baptist preacher and I know something about the Bible."

I thought this was wonderful and so I perked up again. I was ready to start back with the Bible.

He said, "I know enough about the Bible to ask you a few questions on it."

I said, "Well, that's fine."

He said, "You know you're going against the Bible, don't you?"

I said, "Is that right?"

"Yeah, you're going against it."

I said, "Could you be a little specific about that?"

"Yeah, over there in Jeremiah (he quoted the chapter and verse), it says over there, Can the leopard change his spots or the Ethiopian change his skin? You're coming down trying to change—you all will have to excuse this language—you're trying to change these niggers' skin. You're just going against the Bible."

I said, "Now, Mr. Bartlett, we haven't done any skin-changing business. This isn't what we're interested in. I know maybe people on both sides have been doing that, but we're in the heart-changing business, not the skin-changing business, and we believe that God can change even a white man's heart."

"Well," he said, "Do you know what the two foundations of the Bible are?"

I said, "Yes sir."

He said, "What are they?"

I said, "Thou shalt love the Lord thy God with all thy heart, and with all thy mind, and with all thy soul, and with all thy strength; and the second is like unto it, thou shalt love thy white neighbor as thyself."

Well, I set a trap for him, thinking that maybe he would correct me on the way I had misquoted it. Since he was the son of a Baptist preacher, I knew that he knew what the right word was, so I purposely put "white neighbor" in there so that he would have to correct me. But it didn't really say white and that was exactly what I wanted *him* to say. But he thought it sounded so good that he didn't ever correct me. He just responded, "Well, that ain't the two foundations of the Bible."

I said, "Well, now, of course, that's what Jesus thought they were, but you are entitled to your own opinion. I'd like to know what you think they are."

"I think they are the Ten Commandments and the Sermon on the Mount."

"Oh," I said, "I quite agree, I quite agree. But the Ten Commandments and the Sermon on the Mount just spell out these great prophecies, these great commandments. Jesus said on these two, 'I am the law and the prophets.' The law of the Old Testament and the prophetic speaking of the New Testament, too, I suppose is included in the prophecy. So I would include . . . I would say that you are right, so I go along with you."

"All right," he said, "You believe then in the Sermon on the Mount? Don't it say in there something about if a man smites you on the right cheek, you turn to him the other also?"

I said, "Yes, it says that."

He said, "All right, now, if you really believe that, and these folk are shooting at you like you claim they are, blowing up your place and all like that like you claim they are, why don't you just turn the other cheek?"

Well, at that time, there had been twenty-eight attacks on Koinonia with fire, gunshots, dynamite, personal attacks, and other things. And I said, "Mr. Bartlett, we have turned the left cheek, the right cheek, both hind ones. We have turned every cheek we've got. What do you do when you run out of cheeks?"

I said, "But maybe you need to be reminded of that other foundation of the Bible, the Ten Commandments, and as I recall, one of them in there says something to this effect: 'Thou shalt not kill'."

I said, "Brother, do you believe that?"

He kind of hung his head, and I said, "If you believe in the foundations of the Bible, especially this one, why don't you get these people who are trying to kill our little children and trying to kill us, and bring them in here and tell them that the laws of God and the laws of this country say thou shalt not kill?"

Well, I have taken so much of your time I want to give you a chance now to raise questions about this. I tried to speak to you from not a theological abstraction but an exhortation situation, and I am ready to say, on the basis of all this experience, that I believe more deeply than ever before, and I am ready to commit myself more deeply now than I have ever committed myself, that there is no other way than that given through Jesus Christ our Lord two thousand years ago.

What are some of your questions? I have about ten or fifteen minutes left, I think.

Question: "Is your position in accord with the Southern Baptist Convention?"

On what issue? No, really, I've never made that the slightest interest on my part. I have never committed myself to the Southern Baptist Convention. My commitment is to God in Jesus Christ, and if the Southern Baptists walk that way, then I shall have fellowship with them; if they don't, I will not have fellowship with them. I don't think this at all represents the position of Southern Baptists in general. It represents the position of some Southern Baptists, but in general, no.

Question: "Are you opposed to all forms of violence?"

I'm not opposed to some forms of violence. I reared my children with a certain amount of violence. That's why that part of the anatomy particularly is created—for the reception of violence.

Question: "Did not Jesus use force or violence to drive the money changers out of the temple?"

I don't know that he inflicted any kind of punishment on them. Did he abuse their bodies in any way? No, I don't think we can infer from the Scriptures that he struck any of them. As well as I get it, he upturned the table and turned the money over, and that was worse than striking them, I suppose. But so far as I can get from the story, he did not physically inflict any damage or harm on those people. Now you might have a different version, but I do not find it. The Pharisees, when they got on the outside, they didn't ask him how he did it. They said by what authority did you cast aside, so I presume that he cast them out not with violence but authority.

Question: "How did you come to establish Koinonia Farm?"

Well, we didn't sit down and map it out. It was a matter of trying to find the will of God and to give ourselves to it. It wasn't a matter of manipulating God and saying, "Look, God, I just invented an eight-point record system and I'd like for you to come in on it." It wasn't that kind of a thing, but more of an effort of what is God up to? What is he trying to do? What are his redemptive purposes for mankind now? How can I, God, be used by you for the accomplishment of those purposes? So really trying to discern the will of God as clearly as we could—and it's always a difficult thing—and to let ourselves be used and expendable in his hands to accomplish his purposes. Now, of course, we knew it was dangerous. I was born and raised right down there in South Georgia. I know that the boiling point of some of those folks is about 35 degrees below zero, especially on this point. I've had dealings with them. I'm no ignoramus. But, at the same time, I felt that the teachings of God in Christ clearly cut diametrically opposite of Southern conditions and so I had to choose to which I would give my loyalty. I knew that it was dangerous to give my loyalty to God but I also knew it was more dangerous not to. And this is what a lot of folks leave out. I have seen men, liberal ministers, utterly destroyed on this issue. And I thank God that he gave me the opportunity to have the physical danger that I've been through without the awful, awful spiritual danger. Jesus said don't be a-scared of those folks who can kill the body, that's nothing, as long as it's somebody else's body, you know. He said don't be scared of those folks that can kill the body, but I'll tell you who to be scared of, you be scared of that fellow who can destroy both body and soul in Gehenna. I tell you be afraid of him.

Chapter 4

Koinonia in Transition

[This lecture and the one presented in chapter 3 are from the Gheens Lectures delivered by Clarence Jordan during October 1968 at the Southern Baptist Theological Seminary. Both this and the previous lecture were transcribed from a tape recording.]

* * *

In the class yesterday afternoon, I told you that I would continue what I had given yesterday—telling you something about the transition that is taking place at Koinonia and the projection of these ideas which I outlined to you, lifting them out of a little pilot project type of thing and making them into more of a movement affair. Now, in doing that, I do not mean to imply that these ideas or this method of Christian community was invalid; it's just that times have changed so that we have to be flexible enough to fit ourselves, our programs, our approaches, our ideas into this changing affair. What was valid—and I think Koinonia *was* valid during the 40s and 50s—we greatly needed to have an integrated Christian witness in the midst of the very segregated society, and we intend to continue that witness. But, as a little group of people—as a beachhead, so to speak—we *now* feel that to continue just as a little beachhead, a little isolated group in the midst of south Georgia, would be to sit on the bank of the stream and watch the currents of history just move on off and leave you.

Now, religious people particularly are prone to crystallization. We tend to fossilize. We get a big idea and we think that it's wonderful, and we just hold on to it long after history has moved on off and left us. I think this was a problem of religious people in Jesus' day. He blasted the professional ecclesiastics because, he said, "You are like graves which appear not and men walk over you unawares [Luke 11:44]."

Now in the Greek, it reads literally, "You are like graves of which there is no longer any evidence." Have you ever been to an old-time cemetery where they didn't have any tombstones or anything, and they just covered you up? The fresh dirt soon becomes old dirt and the pine straw falls on it and covers it. And pretty soon, you just can't tell where there was a grave at all.

And he said, "You folks have been dead and buried so long that there is not even any fresh dirt as evidence of your funeral. And, more than that, people just walk over you without being aware that there's a corpse buried there. At one time, you at least had the capacity to raise a stink, but you have even lost that. You are just that relevant. You are as relevant as a corpse, dead and buried for forty or fifty years, and there is not even any evidence of you. And folks walk all over you without even hearing a prophetic note out of you."

Now we Christians have to beware of fossilization. Preachers have to beware. We have to be ready for change. And so Koinonia, I think, and its old regime has served its day just as the horse and buggy served its day. I was on the verge of just saying, Well, I have about made my contribution to society, and I'll just retire now and go around and lecture about history and past events. And I really didn't see any future for Koinonia other than just folding it up. But about two years ago, a young fellow come there named Millard Fuller. He is from Montgomery, Alabama. He drove up in a *great big* Lincoln Continental and was going to spend about an hour greeting his friend, Al Henry, who was living at Koinonia. I didn't even know Millard. We were all sitting at the community tables there. I was sitting at one; this fellow and his friend Al were sitting at the other; and I got into a discussion with a Catholic priest and the managing editor of the *Columbus Enquirer* about possessions. This editor said, "You know, our people over in Columbus—our wealthy people—don't have a sense of stewardship. They just want to make all the money they can get."

And I said, "Well, that seems to be typical of wealthy people. They are money addicts. They're just like folks who have been hitting the bottle. They have already had more than it takes to make them drunk but they just can't quit. They want more. So quit drinking. They're still thirsting for money. They're just . . . I call them 'money-ics'."

This guy was sitting right back of me who had driven up in his big Lincoln Continental and I noticed that he was leaning over *real far* to hear me talking about moneyism. After it was over, he said, "Can I talk with you?"

And I said, "Buddy, I tell ya, I am awful busy. We are right in the middle of our mail orders (it was just about Christmastime) and I got to go to work. But if you stay over tonight, I will talk with you."

He said, "Well, I was just going to stay about a half-hour and have lunch with you."

I said, "Well, I'm too busy. I gotta go. If you can stay the night, OK."

"So, well, will you let me stay the night?"

And I said, "Of course we will. We'll put you up."

So we put him up in a little ole house out there that had about fifty-some-odd bullet holes in it where we put all our guests! And so he decided to stay over. That night, he came up to me and he was gnawing on his finger. He had just about gnawed his fingernail off. He was kinda panting and he said nervously, "You know," he said, "I think I am a money-addict."

And I said, "How bad are you addicted?"

"Well," he said, "my salary this year—not counting my extra bonuses and everything—was greater than that of the president of the United States."

I said, "It's almost up to mine, isn't it?" (I thought he was pulling my leg! I hadn't even seen his Continental.)

And he said, "Yeah, it was. I had one big ambition in life and that was to make a million dollars. I graduated from the University of Alabama three years ago and I made my million. Already made my million dollars."

So I said, "Whoo, man, you really *are* addicted aren't you?"

He said, "I just feel like I got something on my chest. I can hardly breathe."

I said, "A million dollars on your chest, man, I don't see how you get a breath at all."

So, we talked on and on and the man stayed for a solid month and, at the end of the month (or during that month), he had done what Jesus told the rich young ruler to do but he wouldn't do. He sold all of his possessions and gave it to the poor. He gave away the whole million dollars.

Now that young fellow decided then he wanted to give his life to Jesus Christ. But Jesus didn't *just* say, "Sell what thou hast and give it to the poor." He said, "Come and follow me." And so, he wanted to give his life. So he got him a job raising money for a little Negro college near Jackson, Mississippi—Tougaloo Development Committee, raising money, very successfully, for that college.

Back in May, he wrote me a very short note. He said, "I've just resigned my job with Tougaloo College. What you got up *your* sleeve?" Well, I didn't have anything up my sleeve. I was ready to fold up Koinonia. I had already told folks I was leaving. I had been offered a job teaching and had just about gotten ready to accept it. So he wrote and asked me, "What you got up your sleeve?" And I said, "I've got *nothing* up my sleeve. Nothing whatsoever. And I'm thinking about quitting this thing."

And then I thought, "Now, wait a minute. God might have something up his sleeve." I had been tremendously concerned about events and things that were happening in Sumter County and happening all over the nation. And so I said, "Maybe you and I ought to get together and talk."

So he flew down from New York and I met him in Atlanta and we spent the whole day talking and praying together. From it emerged a whole new vision of what *could* happen. Many of these things I had hoped could take place, but I saw no way of implementing them. He came with his brilliant imagination, his great business sense, and, coupled with what little theology I might have, some great ideas came to us.

Now, before going into that, I would like to point out a little bit to you what *is* happening in the world today. We are concerned about the urban area, we're concerned about the ghetto, but the real answer to this problem might also be concerned with the rural areas. I don't think we are going to be able to find an adequate solution to the city apart from the country and the country apart from the city.

Now I want to tell you what is happening right in my county, and I think this is typical of the whole region that I live in, not only Georgia, but Alabama, and Mississippi, and South Carolina, the whole South in general. First, there has been a tremendous migration of people away from the rural areas into the cities. Here are some statistics for our own county.

In 1930, there were 15,509 people living in the rural areas in Sumter County. Of that number, 4,000 were white, approximately 12,000 were black. That is, there were three Negroes to each white man living in the rural area.

Thirty years later (in 1960), instead of 15,000 people in the rural area, there were 5,000—a reduction of 300%—and, of that number, slightly over 1,600 of them were white and just about slightly over 3,000 of them were black. That is, 9,000 Negroes had left Sumter County in thirty years. The population had gone down that much and the increase of that population had also gone.

Now where had they gone? Well, I know where they had gone. They had gone to Hartford, Connecticut. There are today more Negroes in Hartford, Connecticut, from Sumter County than there are Negroes *in* Sumter County. They all moved to Hartford.

Now why did they go to Hartford? They went to Hartford just for the same reason that all migrations go. Somebody goes, gets a job, they write back to their aunts, their uncles, nephews, nieces, their cousins, and pretty soon their relatives start coming up there. Then *their* relatives start coming and a flow of migration goes to a certain point. You can trace it.

Certain cities in Mississippi have their counterparts in the north. Hartford considers herself the sister city of Americus since just about all of this surplus—people who have been pushed off of the farms—have gone to Hartford, Connecticut.

Now Hartford, Connecticut, not only gets practically all of the *people* from Sumter County; they also get nearly all the *money* from Sumter County. We not only send our *people* to Hartford, we send our *money* to Hartford. I know, because we send *our* annual tribute up there. Koinonia sends an annual tribute of about $2,000 every year to Hartford, Connecticut. In fact, I would say that half of the farmers in Sumter County send a rather sizable contribution every year to Hartford, Connecticut. Why? Well, because an insurance company is headquartered up there named John Hancock. Did you ever hear of John Hancock? It owns about half of Sumter County. Got mortgage on it. And they let us out for a little word called *interest*. They are very *interested* in Sumter County. And another company that is tremendously interested in Sumter County is the Prudential Company. Now Prudential understands. I mean it *understands,* how to keep people poor. And these big companies that lend out the money are the ones to whom you pay your annual tribute.

Now to get a little specific about it: Next to us is a farmer named Rob Hamilton. We've helped Rob a good bit over the years. We helped him as a little old tenant farmer when he didn't have anything but a one-eyed old mule that wasn't worth a thing. He kept him anyway. Old Rob tells that one time he put the old mule up for collateral. The banker said, "Describe him."

He said, "Well, he is lame in his front leg, got a broke hind leg, blind in both eyes and ain't got no teeth."

The banker said, "Rob, what in the world are you keeping a mule like that for?"

He said, "For collateral."

Again, let me read you a few statistics in our county. In 1930, the average value of a farm in Sumter County was $3,290. That is, if you had $3,000, you could buy you a farm free from all debt and go into farming. Way back yonder in the early forties, I had a fellow ask me, he said, "I got about $2,000. I want to go into farming. What do you think is the best way to invest it? Should I buy a mule, should I buy a wagon, what should I buy with my $1,500 to $2,000?" I drew him up a list of what I thought were priorities.

But *now*, if he were to come to me and say he's got $2,000, he wants to get started farming, what's the best way to invest it, I'd tell the young fellow, "The best thing to do with that $2,000 is to use it to court a gal that's got $150,000."

Because here is what has happened thirty years later: the average value of that farm in 1960 is $61,218. In 1968, the average value of a farm in Sumter County is right at $137,000. Now what's happened to Rob? He's had to keep up with this thing. He's had to automate his poultry operation. He's had to get big tractors, he's had to get big corn combines, all that kind of stuff. How did he get this extra capital to keep his farm? He got it from John Hancock. John Hancock loves to let you have capital. Because it's a very nice thing to let farmers have. Now Rob's investment is right at $130,000—let's knock it off and say $120,000—and he is paying Prudential eight percent on about $40,000 of it; he's paying some of the others seven and one-half percent. Let's average it out at eight percent which is quite common. One hundred twenty thousand dollars at eight percent is $9,600 *interest*. Do you get that? That's how much he's got to pay these folks who come around for their annual tribute. Now Rob's got 300 acres of land. If Rob were to plant the whole 300 acres (which he couldn't do because fifty acres of it is marginal land—he might squeeze out 250 acres)—but let's say he put the whole 300 acres in corn and he got the average of the state of Georgia—forty bushels to the acre—on 300 acres, Rob would make 12,000 bushels of corn. You know what corn is bringing right now? The December futures on corn is $1.03¾ per bushel. Because it is going to cost you three and three-quarters cents to haul it to the folks you are going to give it to, you've got approximately $1.00 a bushel. If you produced 12,000 bushels, that is $12,000, out of which you've got to pay your seed, fertilizer, tractor maintenance, implements, and all that kind of stuff. I know what the average profit on a bushel of corn is after you have paid all your expenses. It is approximately thirty cents a bushel. If he made 12,000 bushels, that means he made $3,600. And John Hancock's coming around saying "Buddy, you owe me $9,600 *interest.*"

There never was a time in all of history that I can read where the feudal barons took *all* of a man's crop and then made him borrow some more from them to pay him off like we're doing now. We are destroying our farmers and doing it rather rapidly. So Rob is going into bankruptcy. He's selling his farm and he's moving to town and the Negro who is living with him will be moving to Hartford.

Now is there any alternative to this? Is there some way out of it? Can we break this awful oppression?

Well, I think that we can, but I believe that it's going to call for a new spirit. And this is why Koinonia now is thinking in terms of a projection in three directions. And you will recognize these immediately as the directions that Jesus took for his ministry: a ministry of preaching, a ministry of teaching, and a ministry of healing. These are not to run consecutively but concurrently—all together; not one preceding because we feel that the most urgent need of mankind today is a change in his attitude, a restructuring of his life along the lines of the gospel. He needs so radically and so desperately to do what Jesus told the people they had to do, and that is repent. Jesus began his whole ministry before he healed anybody. He started off by saying, "The Kingdom of God is at hand: repent ye, and believe in the gospel." That is, "Resturcture your whole way of thinking and living, for a new order of God is impinging upon you. You have to restructure your life to fit it in with this new order."

Now John the Baptist started his ministry with the same thing. These great prophets felt that it is absolute idiocy to talk about changing the world without changing people. Now let me read you what old John the Baptist did.

I want to read a little bit from Luke 3 here. I think this is a wonderful bit of ethics here. In the third chapter of Luke, beginning with the first verse, we have these words.

Now in the fifteenth year of the reign of Tiberius Caesar while Pontius Pilate was governor over Judea and while Herod was tetrarching over Galilee and Philip his brother was tetrarching over Iturea and Trachonitis, while Lysanias was still holding out over Abilene, and during the high priesthood of Annas and Caiaphas, the word of God came to John, Zach's boy, down on the farm.

Now, you see the humor here that the Roman emperor . . . here are all those big governors, here are the two big high priests ("the co-presidents of the Southern Baptist Convention"), *all* of the Big Brass assembled—the whole power structure assembled—and you expect the word of God to come plunking down right into the middle of the power structure. But does it? It just goes right on over to that little old boy John, Zach's boy, down on the farm. I think you'd call this the first New Testament "passover," *all the way over*! It passed by the big insurance office buildings. It went all the way by the governors' mansions. It just bypassed the *whole* power structure and went to the little folks.

So that little old boy, John, Zach's boy, got to preaching around. He went all around the country preaching a baptism . . . of what? Of repentance, of restructuring your life. And he took his text, like all great prophets did, including the Master himself, from Isaiah.

Here is what he said.

There's a voice shouting in the wilderness, Prepare the way of the Lord. Make his paths straight. Every valley shall be filled in, and every mountain and hill shall be brought low, and the crooked shall be straightened out, and the *trakia*—little minor corrugations—shall be made exceedingly smooth, and all humanity shall see the salvation of God.

You get the picture there now? This old John is out there, he's saying the mountains shall be brought down, the overfill from the mountains shall be put in the valleys, the valleys shall be brought up, and the crooks shall all be straightened out. That's *really* going to be a job. And then, even the little minor irregularities are going to be straightened out, the *trakia*. Any of you folks ever been out on a country dirt road where it has been scraped by the road machine and they call it a washboard? Not even going to allow—not the big mountains and the valleys—but not even the little old corrugations in this highway of the Lord. It's going to be straight smooth. So here you're getting the mountains bulldozed off and the valleys filled in and roads straightened. We call this guy John the Baptist. We ought to call him John the Bulldozer, out there straightening up, making a path for the Lord in society, making his path smooth and level.

So then he began to say to those who came out to be baptized by him, "You sons of snakes!" Now that's proper language to folks who live in these big office buildings. "You sons of snakes!" Now I don't recommend that you begin a revival addressing your congregation like that, nor that you do it to preach in your trial sermon. But "You sons of snakes"—and let's do keep it snakes—"who warned you to flee from the impending fury? You start making fruits that are compatible with *metanoia*—with a changed way of life—and don't you start giving me any of that 'we good white folks' stuff." (In the Greek, it's "We got Abraham for a daddy.") "Don't you give me that Abraham-daddy stuff. So I want to tell you that God is able to make children of Abraham out of these stones. If he just wanted folks with the proper genealogy, he could pick him up any old rocks and make him some folks out of them." (I think he did.) "Already the chain saw is lying at the root of the trees and every tree that does not make good fruit is chopped down and thrown into the fire." That is, every institution, whether it be governmental, economic, or otherwise, that does not exist for the welfare of mankind shall be chopped down, sawed down, and let to fall and hear the mighty voice of history shout, "Timber!"

I tell you there is going to be a lot of timber falling unless we get on with this *metanoia* pretty quick. We've built our trees up mighty high, and history, the old chain saw, is rasping and gnawing and pulling the sawdust down.

And the crowds were saying to him, "What shall we do?"

And he said to them, "He who has two shirts, let him share with him who has no shirt and let him do the same thing with his biscuits."

Now what he is saying there is that the two-shirt man will share with the no-shirt man and there will be two one-shirt men. That is, the overfill from the mountain shall be shared with the valley and they will be brought up level. What he's proclaiming here is an era of equality. And even minor inequities or irregularities will be straightened out.

And he went on with other ways, pointing out how that it was necessary for soldiers to restructure *their* lives, for publicans to restructure *their* lives, for everyone to restructure their lives to fit in with this impinging new order. So I don't see how we can get anywhere without some *real* prophetic preaching today helping people understand what repentance really means and how it means a real *change* of life, maybe changing the standard of living that we have and humbling ourselves and being willing to share with other people.

Now the next point is that of teaching. You do not preach prophetically without expecting somebody to accept the ideas and so you begin to teach and train, "make disciples" as Jesus calls it. And so we are going to be setting up discipleship schools, some of them peripatetic, kind of wandering around from city to city, others will be held at Koinonia. We've already gotten into this. Our first discipleship school was held back in August. We're having another one two weeks from now in which we gather people together to come there to *really* go into the prophetic implications of the gospel, not concerned about the preservation of an ecclesiastical order or a political order or sociological order of any kind, but trying to find out what the purposes and mind of God are for man at this particular juncture of history.

We'll be having other discipleship schools in cities throughout the United Staes and I will be giving a good bit of my time to that. Already I am being released from my farm duties. Others have taken over the job of milking cows, making hay, and much of the actual farm work that I have been doing, and I will be moving from Americus—from Koinonia—up around Atlanta so that I will be near the airport and other means of communication and transportation so that I can devote myself almost entirely to the ministry of preaching and teaching. There will be a larger staff—we're already forming that—of men who will be engaged in this with me, a team-type thing of six or eight men, in the early stages of it, devoting themselves to teaching and preaching.

Then that brings us to this: there is no point to preach to a man, there is no point to teach him, unless he takes what has been preached to him and what has been taught him and begins to apply it, and this is what we call "application" or "healing." Now by healing we do not mean just the healing of the body. It means the healing of all the hurt of mankind—economic hurt, racial hurt, international hurt, all this kind of thing as well as physical hurt. The whole hurt of mankind is brought into this business of healing and we are to make it whole.

Now in its initial stages we cannot tackle the *whole* hurt of mankind, but we're already at work on three phases of it which later will be expanded. This whole healing thing is what we call "partners": trying to implement the idea of partnership with God and partnership with one another, trying to take this broken, fragmented, anonymous society that we have and create once again the idea of partnership and mutual responsibility and mutual love and mutual respect. So these three things which we call healing will be the partnership idea and there will be partnership-farming, partnership-industries, and partnership-housing.

Now undergirding all of that is a fund which we call the Fund for Humanity. Now the reason we have to have this fund is because of these figures which I have cited. Here's Rob Hamilton. He has no money. He has to get it from John Hancock and Prudential and other sources. Here's the black man that's staying on his farm. He has no inheritance. His father left him just what his grandfather left his father, which was poverty. The only way that a man can really get anything today such as land and so forth is to inherit it. So this fund is to provide an inheritance for the disinherited. Rob is selling his farm. He's had to go out of it, in part—almost entirely—because his creditors have put too great a load of interest upon his back. We are going to buy Rob's farm. We're paying $80,000 for it which we think is a fair and good price. We'll buy the farm—and we already have two partners lined up for it, one a white man, one a black man—and we're saying to them, "This is your inheritance.

Neither of you could inherit it from your earthly father but you are inheriting it from your spiritual father. The land is the Lord's and, as in all inheritances, you do not pay interest. You do not pay principal on it. This is yours. So we're substituting a word that we call 'usership' for 'ownership.' It's not yours to own, but its yours to use for as long as you want to use it. When you make 12,000 bushels of corn, you don't have to pay Hancock or Prudential anything. You make it by the sweat of your brow and it's yours—all 12,000 bushels of it. It's yours, but, out of gratitude for what others have done for you, you should be willing to share; and, out of grace and gratitude, you should be willing to give something to the Fund for Humanity."

We've already got another pair of farmers lined up. Plez Nelson has been over and he wants a farm. He's a good farmer but he's about to be forced out just like Rob Hamilton is. We can save him. We can put him a partner with him. His land now has a heavy mortgage on it, and he is bearing it just overwhelmingly, hardly has anything left for his children by the time he pays that interest. We'll pay off the note and say then, "Plez, it's clear now and it's yours, whatever you make on it, but you should give something to the Fund for Humanity."

Now this is the real clue, I think, to the success of this thing. It is not like a government handout. You give nobody nothing; you just take the foot off of his neck. You're not training him in dependency like many government programs do in which it trains them just to be parasites—"Give me, give me, give me." It isn't helping people even to help themselves. It's helping people to help *others* and keeping that vision alive, and I think it's going to give a motivation—already is doing so—that just making money by itself does not have.

This young business executive I mentioned, he's getting a wonderful joy out of giving his great abilities to these partnership industries and I want to tell you about that. We got leftovers from Koinonia which have been donated to the Fund for Humanity. We got a pretty thriving pecan-shelling plant. We got a fruitcake bakery. We got a candy kitchen, all of these doing pretty good business, a profitable business.

Incidentally, I guess I can pause here for this commercial. Any of you-all need any pecans or fruitcake or candy for Christmas, why, you drop us a line and we would be glad to send you the price list for it and you order from us. Pecans are one of Georgia's number one products and, in fact, Georgia is the nut-producing state of the union. That is, pecans, peanuts, and things like that, you know. And we are on a campaign to get as many nuts out of Georgia as we can (leaving, of course, enough to assemble the legislature).

These things are already in operation and they will be operated the same way we do the farmers. There is no capital. You don't buy stock. It's yours for an inheritance. You don't have to go to sending off your big annual tribute up to John Hancock and Prudential so they can get up on their high office buildings and look down on their domain.

Now, we started this with a high school boy this year and he's a promising kid. He wants to go to college. He has no money to go to college. He had no money to go into business. So we allocated him some land. We bought him some steers to go on it. He went in a cattle-feeding operation and he's done *quite well* with it. He's giving part of what he's made to the Fund for Humanity so that others can go into it. Now, he's getting him another high school kid to be his partner and we're going to *really* put them into it this year. We're allocating them a hundred acres of fine coastal bermuda grass pasture. We're going to stock it with two hundred steers, going to cost about $20,000. These kids are going to have quite a bit of investment then, but there won't be any interest, no rent on the land. If they did it the old way, they would give off about, oh, practically all of it to others who are eating their flesh and taking the rewards of their labor. Under this plan my prediction is (according to what is done this year), next year, off of that two hundred acres, they should make a profit between them of somewhere around $6,000. Now, if they did it under the old system, I venture to say they would have done well to break even. This way, it is just about equal to what the interest would have been, but this is *clear*. They are going to have $6,000. Now, these kids are already talking about how much they are gonna want to give to the Fund for Humanity. They are going to take a little bit, lay it aside. I am predicting that they'll give half of it. We are not teaching this. We are teaching them to give according as the Lord hath prospered. And according to the grace that's in your heart. And I venture to say these two high school kids are going to split that half—they are going to give $3,000 of it to the Fund for Humanity and then they will split the other $3,000 between themselves and they will have $1,500 apiece to go into their college education fund.

The poor really don't need charity. They need capital. They don't need caseworkers. They need coworkers. They need somebody to work *with* them. Somebody to help them, somebody not to exploit them, somebody to help to get these big fat greasy folks' foot off of their necks so that they can stand up and be human beings and not exploited bits of property. This is all they need. And then they need to learn how to help, once you get on your feet, to strengthen your brethren. They need to know how to act as a man of grace sharing gladly and from your heart that which the Lord has provided for you.

Now we're doing the same thing with housing. We've laid off forty-two half-acre plots. It's our experience that white or black people do not leave rural areas until life becomes either intolerable or impossible, and we are trying to make life not only tolerable and possible but enjoyable and pleasant. One of the reasons they leave is because they can get no land; nobody will sell to them. Nobody will share with them so we are making available forty-two half-acre plots for these people. It's big enough for a house and big enough for a garden and for a little chicken house. And then we're helping them get jobs also. Now we have found that we can get for $5,500 a four-bedroom house, brand new, with a bathroom and a kitchen and a living room all for $5,500 with the key complete. Now we are dividing these forty-two plots into two sections. There is one big area that will be allocated for common property for the whole group for recreation, a big plot in the center in which there will be ball diamonds, recreational equipment, we hope someday a swimming pool, and all that kind of stuff, grounds for picnicing. That will be common property; it will belong to the whole group. Around that will be all of these houses, these little homesteads.

We're dividing it into two for experimental purposes. Twenty lots are being sold outright to people at a very nominal sum. These half-acre homesteads we're selling to them for somewhere between $75 and $100. They can pay on it a dollar or two at the time or ten to fifteen dollars at the time. Now we are saying to them, "You go through the normal channels of financing." Some of them want to try it on their own and we say, "Fine, that's good. You go right on. You go up to Mr. John Hancock and tell them you want the money to put your house up. He'll put it up for you and I'll tell you what your payments are going to be on that $5,500 house. It's going to be $57.43 per month. That's how much you're going to have to pay with interest."

Now the other twenty-two [plots] down below this area will be done on the koinonia principle, on the partnership principle. The Fund for Humanity will put the house up and say to the family, "We're not giving you this house but, if you pay for a house, you're going to get it. You're not going to have to pay for three in order to get one, which you have to do through the usual channels of financing. We're going to prorate this over twenty years. You'll pay for it, plus a small administration fee of about three dollars a month. Your payments will be $22.08 a month plus three dollars administration fee for bookkeeping and so forth. Twenty-five dollars a month is what you're going to have to pay for yours. These other folks, if they get the identical house with interest will have to pay $57 a month. Now that $35 doesn't seem like much money. But, to people whose income is around $100 a month, that's big money.

Now when we sell this house to this family without any interest, we're still going to say to them, "You know, you received this by grace. Now you should live by grace. You're saving $35 a month on interest. You should be making a contribution to the Fund for Humanity in order that others also may have houses without interest and without having to fatten up somebody who's sucking their blood." So the Fund for Humanity will continue to grow from its industries, from its housing, from its farming.

And then we're hoping also to find a lot of people who will join us who will be willing, wherever they are, to restructure their lives. A man who's making a lot of money these days, he ought to be willing to live much more humbly than he probably is. I know some preachers who could greatly alter their lives and live much more simply and give the surplus away. Augustine has said that, "He who possesses a surplus possesses the goods of others." That's just a polite way of saying, if you've got too much you're a thief. Now there are a lot of thieves going around in the world just simply got too much. They are two-coat people who *ought* to be sharing with the no-coat people. They are the two-biscuit men who ought to be sharing with the no-buscuit people. And so we are going to be superb beggars, I guess you'd call it. Not beggars either because it is more blessed to give than it is to receive—and a man who has the opportunity to give and to share a biscuit, you're not begging anything from him, you're giving him the privilege of investing in humanity rather than squandering it on himself and his children.

I was going to give you some time to ask questions. Our time is gone. We have five minutes? All right. . . .

Question: "What can we do to help Koinonia?"

What are several things you can do? One, we need you. We're going to need a lot of shepherds. We're going to need a lot of spiritually minded people. We're going to need teachers. We're going to need all kinds of people. Going to need practical men who know how to run businesses, farms, and all like that, who can take over these housing projects and many, many other things. You can give us yourselves. And this is the most important thing.

Secondly, this isn't something that just Koinonia can do. This Fund for Humanity and everything is something that anybody can do; it's adaptable anywhere. You could start it here, anywhere.

Thirdly, you maybe got people in your churches who definitely have too much. You may not have any Fund for Humanity set up but you could go to them and say, "Look, brother, don't you think you've got two coats? Can't you get along with one? Why don't you throw the rest of it into either our Fund for Humanity or anybody else's Fund for Humanity, for that matter." In other words, this provides a channel through which people can really share without it being a handout, a "gimme" kind of thing. It's a real channel through which your money can be invested in humanity rather than just given away. I think you could do that.

I think you could find that, many times, the greatest ministry that you could make would be to live as a poor man in an affluent church. Some of you are going to be pastors of affluent churches. I'm quite sure a few of you will be. You've got that look in your eyes. Now one of the greatest witnesses you could be would be a poor man pastoring an affluent church. Take all the salary they give you, but invest it back in humanity.

Question: "Where do you find all the money for all these projects?"
By a counterfeiting operation! . . . No, we are finding people—some of them rather wealthy people—who really are concerned about this and who feel guilty for having so much. They really want a sound, practical, hardheaded business way of handling it, and we are finding people who want to contribute to it. This millionaire, fortunately, he hadn't quite given away all of his million. He'd only gotten rid of $900,000 of it and he still had $100,000 that hadn't been liquidated or designated and he threw that into the Fund for Humanity. I think we now have somewhere close to $350,000 in it, but we are just getting started. I mean the thing hasn't been going but for just a few months. Now this guy, if he could make a million dollars for himself in three years, I've got a hunch he's going to make a million dollars for the Lord in three years. He's got that kind of ability. He just touches stuff and it "Boom!" turns to gold, like that. You oughta have a deacon like that in your church. He just sparkles with ideas. And he's a hard-nosed businessman who knows how to implement his ideas.

Question: "What kind of approach do you use?"
Visitor preaching. You preach it, and then you find somebody who

wants to ask you a question and you let him have it from the shoulder. There are many contacts through preaching and teaching.

Well, I think that is the bell that terminates all good works and I guess we'd better stop right there. I wish we could go on with this. I hope that we will have contact with you because it's a tremendously exciting venture for us and I think it has potential to answer some of the real pressing problems that we have run into in South Georgia. And I think our problems are typical of problems throughout the United States and even throughout the world.

Epilogue

Through the years I have watched the Koinonia experiment take root in Southwest Georgia soil and grow into a tree whose leaves are for the healing of humanity. Clarence Jordan turned his dream into deeds and Koinonia Partners has become internationally as well as nationally known. Thousands visit the farm and experience something of the vision and hope of Clarence as they witness the radical sharing of the people and catch the spirit of the community.

Through the Koinonia experiment, audio taped speeches, and the Cotton Patch Version of the Bible Clarence, though dead, yet speaks to this generation. His is a prophetic word of peace, justice, and love incarnate in human personality and practice.

Appendix 1

Letters

Correspondence
with Clarence

From 1942 until Clarence's death in 1969, we occasionally corresponded with each other. Selected letters throw some light on the early development of Koinonia Farm near Americus, Georgia. They also reveal the courage and the commitment of Christians on the frontiers of faith in action.

Unfortunately, some correspondence with Clarence is missing. In those earlier days, we did not have ready access to copy machines and some correspondence was in handwriting; hence, we did not preserve our communication.

* * *

[The following was part of a letter from Clarence dated 1943, less than a year after the founding of Koinonia Farm. The letter was to our mutual friend Arthur Steilberg, a Louisville contractor and builder, who provided the down payment on Koinonia Farm. Arthur often said, "I don't believe in the economic philosophy of Clarence, but I believe in Clarence." Arthur shared a copy of this letter with me about development at Koinonia Farm, as he also shared other information from Clarence.]

As an alternative to borrowing, we thought of letting friends furnish a cow or calf and we furnish the pasture and care, and divide the profit on the gain. This, however, did never materialize, due to our lack of time to press it.

At one time we had around twenty head of hogs, but due to lack of feed, sold them down to seven. Two sows are to farrow in a week, which will give us all we can handle.

Due to the extreme scarcity of poultry and eggs in this section, and because I majored in poultry in college, and because the farmers here sorely need something besides cotton and peanuts to turn to, we went in rather heavy for chickens. With small, homemade brooders we were so successful in raising our 700 chicks that we've built quite a few brooders for neighbors and their interest in poultry is already increasing. Of our chicks, 500 were pure-bred, high producing Barred Rock pullets, which will begin laying in about six weeks. They consume a sack of feed a day now, and are costing us about $100 a month to feed.

When it came to the matter of housing them, we sent to the College of Agriculture for plans for a 24x60 laying house. It is now completed, being constructed in our spare time. The materials cost us $300, the unpaid bill I previously mentioned, but it is worth fully $500 now. It is of practically same construction of our house, with concrete foundation and dressed lumber. It makes a valuable addition to our farm. If we can get the lumber company to wait, we're hoping to pay for it with the eggs from the hens.

So much for the material side of our project. From the spiritual standpoint, we're having difficulty reminding ourselves that all worthwhile missionary endeavor has required years for laying the groundwork. We have done all we can to win the friendship of the people here. While many are very poor, some are good, substantial, middle-class farmers. They have been most hospitable to us, and have loaned us many a helping hand. We united with a quarter-time country church four miles from here, and incidentally, I have just finished holding a revival meeting there which resulted in six conversions. Thru this church, we're trying to render whatever service we can.

During the winter and spring we had classes for illiterate Negroes, there being five enrolled. The busy crop season necessitated a temporary suspension, but we're hoping to begin again this fall.

In order to explain what two preachers were doing out in the country trying to farm, it was necessary to tell honestly what we had in mind. Because our program included the Negroes, quite a bit of opposition was aroused, it being circulated that Martin was a "foreigner" from Burma and that I was a spy with a German wife. Such people, they said, ought not to be allowed to live in these parts. Several "friends" have come to us to warn us "for our own good." The Negroes on our place have also been given some free advice by whites, but they're still sticking with us. So while there has been some thunder, the lightning hasn't struck. When it will is not for me to say, yet I do hope and pray for more time. Our faith is too weak; our friends too few. But of one thing I am confident: God knows best.

But I have talked too much of what we are doing. I'm anxious to know how you and yours are faring, both materially and spiritually. Have you had many contracts? Please know this: that if business reverses should ever beset you, you have a friend here who will share his last biscuit with you. At least we can scratch something to eat out of the ground here.

And are you happy? Is your faith in the Lord Jesus continuing to abound? I pray that his grace and peace may be shed abroad in your heart.

And your boy—did he enter the service? I'm deeply interested in him. How is Mrs. Steilberg, and the other children? Please take a few minutes and write me, for my love for you and interest in your welfare has never diminished one whit.

Yours in Him,
Clarence

* * *

Sept. 20, 1943

Dear Henlee:

Please do not measure my gratitude by my dilatoriness, for I have not ceased to be thankful for your gift of an acre of Georgia dirt, nor for the interest which you have manifested in me and our work. With me it has been "much thought—no write."

I'm to be in Washington for a week the middle part of October, and there's a possibility that I'll come by Louisville on my way there. If so, I surely want to see you and have a long talk with you.

Everything continues to go well with us, though there's plenty of hard work here. I keep thinking we'll get caught up, but we never do. At any rate, we're getting things in shape now where we'll have more time to do missionary work.

Please remember me to the folks at the mission, and tell them that I frequently think of them and pray for them.

Yours very sincerely,
Clarence

* * *

Nov. 30, 1943

Dear Henlee:

Thanks for the check. I feel almost like Shylock for accepting it—one mission taking money from another. I would have felt better to have made the bike a gift to you all. Maybe when we get this thing on a half-way "break-even" proposition we can return it. . . .

I'm still hoping to get up to Louisville soon. It seems that everything is ag'in my coming that way. But I'll make it somehow—before Christmas, I hope.

Give my regards to all. Be assured of my continued prayers.

Yours very sincerely,
Clarence

* * *

Nov. 1, 1944

Dear Henlee:

It was good to hear from you again, both in your letter and from Gordon Hunter, whom I saw recently. Apparently all is going well, and I rejoice in your good work at Union Gospel Mission in the Haymarket.

It is difficult to tell much about our work here in a letter, but here goes. It was begun two years ago this month, and as you know started from nothing except the promises of the Lord and the good will of lots of friends, both of which have proved to be its greatest assets. The 440-acre farm is located in Sumter Co. in southwest Georgia eight miles from Americus, population 11,000. We paid slightly less than $20 per acre for it, or a total of $8000. All but $3000 of this has been paid. The equipment includes a tractor, disc tiller, harrow, mowing machine, combine, wagon, sawmill, planing mill, and various shop equipment.

Livestock includes two mules, one horse, forty head of cattle, twenty hogs and 400 hens. All of this is paid for.

Since coming here we have built a house at a cost of about $1000, and a poultry house which cost $500. An electric water system has been installed. A 2,000-egg incubator and three electric brooders have recently been purchased at a cost of $335. All told, our assets are approximately $19,000 and the indebtedness is $4000. So much for the financial side.

The acreage consists roughly of 100 acres of woodland (pine, oak, hickory), one hundred and forty acres of pasture and two hundred acres of cultivatable land. Besides the two new buildings mentioned above, there are two other residences, two barns, one corncrib, and shed, all of which are about to fall down. We plan eventually to tear down all the buildings that were here when we came. Since coming here we have terraced all the cultivatable land, having constructed approximately 46,000 feet of terracing. Soil-building crops, rotations, and diversification have a large place in our program. We grow peanuts (twelve tons last year, seventeen tons this year), corn (500 bushels), oats (2,100 bushels), wheat (500 bushels), watermelons (ten tons), and miscellaneous crops like sweet potatoes, peas, etc. Our annual egg production is slightly in excess of 60,000.

The personnel of the farm consists of two Negro families with a total of twelve counting children; my family (four in all) and a young fellow named Harry Atkinson from Stetson University in Deland, Florida. Martin England's family was here until two months ago when they were called back into active service in anticipation of being sent back to Burma.

Now, what do we do besides farm? Preaching in country churches, revival meetings, VBS, and outside speaking engagements consume about one-third of my time. During the summer a Southwestern Seminary student stayed with us and organized about twelve white boys for Bible and mission study, recreation, etc. During the school year we transport Negro children to and from their school. Incidentally, we now have $700 cash on hand toward the purchase of a school bus for them.

The Negro Baptist church near here burned down last month, and our sawmill will be used to saw logs to build another. We have organized an interracial Sunday School, which meets here. So far, the only whites to attend are those of us on the farm. We also have a community singing once a week, and I'm trying to teach them to sing by notes.

Later on we're hoping that a doctor will be added to the staff, as well as some teachers. Then we'll need somebody to head up the cooperatives which already are slowly taking shape. But maybe we'd better not talk about our dreams.

On the side we're experimenting with the principles of common ownership and distribution according to need. It's yet to be seen how we come out with this.

If you still have any questions, Henlee, I don't mind answering them. I'm sure you'll do a great job teaching when your turn comes. Just wish I could be there. Since I can't, perhaps you can pass along to us any ideas from others which might be helpful to our enterprise.

> Best regards to all,
> Clarence

* * *

December 4, 1967

Dear Clarence,

Just a note to inquire as to whether or not you will be in these parts this academic year. It has been a long time since you spoke in my classes here at the Seminary. I would like very much to invite you to speak to these classes when you are in this area.

As you know, we have no honorarium for this sort of service. We could have lunch!

Let me hear from you and all about what is going on at the farm.

Recently I preached at Pleasure Ridge Baptist Church and had lunch with our mutual friend, Arthur Steilberg. Wish you could have been there.

With warmest personal regards to you and yours, I remain.

Faithfully yours,
Henlee H. Barnette

* * *

January 25, 1968

Dear Henlee:

I appreciated your letter and especially the invitation to speak to your classes. I have checked through my schedule and at present I don't find anything that would put me in your vicinity. I surely will keep this in mind though and will let you know if anything develops.

It would certainly do me good to sit down for a long chat with you. One of the most difficult things about being stuck off down here in Southwest Georgia is the lack of any real stimulating challenging conversation. Maybe we'll have to plan to get you down here someday.

Thanks again, Henlee, for your kind invitation. I pray God's blessings upon you and wish you much joy and peace.

Yours sincerely,
Clarence

* * *

May 7, 1968

Dear Clarence:

I have been authorized by the theological division of the Southern Baptist Seminary to invite you to give the Gheens Lectures for 1968. We are hoping that you can be on our campus Monday, September 30 through October 2, or Monday, October 14 through 16, or Monday, October 21 through 23, 1968.

Your schedule would be as follows:

Monday: Meet with the faculty club members at 6:00 to 8:30 p.m. In this meeting you would speak more or less informally on a topic of your choice.

Tuesday: Meet the combined Christian Ethics classes at 11:00 a.m. and graduate club for dinner at 6:00 p.m.

Wednesday: Speak in chapel—9:30 a.m., and then meet the combined Christian Ethics class again at 11:00 a.m.

The honorarium would be $300.00 plus expenses. We do hope we can work this program into your busy schedule.

With warmest personal regards, I remain

> Sincerely yours,
> Henlee Barnette

* * *

May 15, 1968

Dear Henlee:

Those Gheens lectures sound like some mighty high cotton for a pea-picking farmer like me, and I'm sorta scared to tackle it. But at the same time, because of our personal friendship, I do not feel disposed to decline it. So if September 30-October 2 will suit you, you can count me in.

You might need to give me a little guidance as to the nature and type of thing that might be expected, as well as any other suggestions which might be helpful to me in making preparation for it.

It will surely be good to have a chance to chew the fat with you again, and you may be sure I'll be anticipating it no end.

Best regards always,
Clarence

* * *

September 10, 1968

Dear Clarence:

We are looking forward to your visit here on campus. So far I have worked out the following schedule for:

Monday, September 30, an informal speech to the Faculty Club. We will have dinner about six o'clock and then turn the meeting over to you.

Tuesday, October 1, a lecture in Christian Ethics 91. This is the introductory course and you may feel free to speak on any subject from air pollution to the Vietnam War.

Wednesday, October 2, speak in Chapel at 10:00 a.m. You will have thirty minutes for this before the chimes go off! It will take us about ten minutes to get ready, if things go as they usually do. So I would suggest that you have a twenty-five minute speech.

Wednesday, October 2, lecture again in Christian Ethics at one o'clock. You will be staying in the Faculty Center right next to the chapel.

Also, I want to work out a luncheon with the faculty on one of these days that you will be here. This will not involve any speech making. Just dialogue.

With warmest personal regards, I remain

Faithfully yours,
Henlee Barnette

* * *

September 14, 1968

Dear Henlee:

The schedule you have worked out looks good, and even I should be able to stay within range of subjects you have mentioned. Maybe the most important topic will be air pollution, that is, the air pollution that takes place nearly every Sunday morning around 11:00!

I'll be leaving Atlanta on Monday, September 30, at 3:10 p.m. and will arrive in Louisville at 4:09 p.m. It probably will be more convenient for you if I take a cab from the airport to the seminary. This should put me there in plenty of time for the six o'clock dinner meeting.

Use your own judgement as to how many extra assignments you give me. I'm fairly rugged and can take a pretty good load, though I would think that three or four shots a day would be sufficient. The idea of an evening session to take the place of many smaller ones might be good, though perhaps not as effective. It would need to be on Tuesday night, as I'll need to leave Wednesday afternoon in time to speak in Evansville, Indiana, that night.

Best regards,
Clarence

* * *

October 16, 1968

Dear Clarence:

Let me express my personal appreciation to you again for your recent visit to our campus in connection with the Gheens Lectures. You received one of the finest responses that has ever been given to a Gheens Lecturer by the student body and faculty. We worked you pretty hard but it was in response to the demand of the students. You forced us to think out what it means to be an authentic Christian in the world today. Some permanent impressions were left upon all of us which we hope will bear fruit in the future.

Please let us have your expense account and we will reimburse you and send you an honorarium as stipulated in our correspondence.

Also, send me information concerning the master's thesis at the University of Georgia dealing with Koinonia Farm. Any other materials on this line which you know about, we would like to have for our library.

Also, send me information concerning what you have good to eat in terms of pecans, fruit cakes, et cetera. Such things make nice Christmas gifts.

Give my best regards to your good wife. I regret that she was not able to accompany you to Louisville.

With warmest personal regards and deepest appreciation I remain

Gratefully,
Henlee Barnette

* * *

October 17, 1968

Dear Bishop of the Hay Market and other Regions:

It was really great to be with you again. Every moment was stimulating, and will be long remembered. It was especially enjoyable to be in your home and to meet your lovely family. I both rejoice and take pride in you all and your faithfulness to Christ.
Enclosed is the paper I should have left with you.

With much love and high esteem,
Clarence

* * *

November 12, 1968

Dear Clarence:

A thousand thanks for the box of wonderful goodies. It was so thoughtful of you to send us the pecans and candy. Needless to say, we enjoyed them very much and all of us express our appreciation.

Hope all is going well with you at the farm. Give my best regards to your loved ones.

We are still discussing the challenging messages which you brought to us in connection with the Gheens Lectures. It just about boils down to a modern paraphrase of Shakespeare: "To Be A Christian Or Not To Be A Christian. That Is The Question."

With warmest personal regards, I remain

Gratefully,
Henlee Barnette

* * *

Letters

Correspondence with Florence

[Correspondence with Florence Jordan is chosen from a number of letters on different subjects. Those selected focus on the formation and function of the Clarence Jordan Institute at the Southern Baptist Theological Seminary, Louisville, Kentucky. After Clarence died, Florence studiously avoided trying to be the matriarch of the Koinonia community. But she remained a model of faith, hope, and love for the fellowship until her death in 1987.]

November 4, 1969

Dear Florence:

I was genuinely grieved to hear of the death of Clarence. As I to you by telephone, I felt that I had lost one of my own brothers. I thaı God upon every remembrance of him.

Yesterday here at Southern Seminary we had a brief memori service for Clarence in the chapel. Fortunately we taped some of ł Gheens Lectures. I plan to play these in some of my classes next wee I am doing this at the request of the students.

Be assured of my heartfelt sympathy in your time of sorrow.

Sincerely,
Henlee Barnette

* * *

April 22, 1970

Dear Florence:

Recently I sent to you data concerning the establishment of the Clarence Jordan Institute of Christian-Ethical Concerns. Also, I indicated that the local committee requested that you serve on the steering committee at large.

I am writing you now because we are in the process of completing a brochure and we would like to have the names of all the members of the steering committee in the brochure.

If you have any reluctance to serve in this capacity, please do not hesitate to say so. We will certainly understand your feelings in this matter.

Today I heard the good news that Dallas Lee is going to join Koinonia Partners. He is a very fine person with administrative and leadership ability. I am sure he will make a real contribution to the wonderful work which you are doing there in Americus.

With warmest personal regards, I remain

Sincerely,
Henlee Barnette

* * *

April 27, 1970

Dear Henlee:

I am sorry that I did not realize it had taken me so long to make up my mind. There has been no definite clarity in mind and I have hesitated to answer yes or no.

The idea of the institute is good and naturally it is gratifying to think that you all think enough of Clarence and his work to undertake such a memorial. I appreciate being asked to take part in the work, but I am reluctant to be a part of it. Please understand that this does not mean that I am not in favor of such a concern being presented to the students. I am just not sure that this is for me.

If this institute is something that God can use, you will find the means of implementing it . . . this my experience has taught me.

I hope all goes well for you personally and will try to call you if and when I am in Louisville.

Cordially,
Florence Jordan

* * *

October 10, 1972

Dear Florence:

During his recent visit to Southern Baptist Seminary, Mr. LaDon Sheats [a resident at Koinonia Farm] informed the steering committee of the Clarence Jordan Institute that our policy of an endowment to memorialize Clarence was a basic contradiction to his economic philosophy.

By common consent the committee agreed that I should write you about this matter. They agreed that if the Clarence Jordan Institute as now structured financially is an embarrassment to you that we should try to find some way to alter the policy.

It is my personal conviction that a memorial does not have to involve all of the ideas of the one being memorialized.

The steering committee would like to have your view on this problem.

Best wishes always,
Henlee Barnettee, chairman
Clarence Jordan Institute

* * *

October 29, 1972

Dear Henlee:

I am sorry that it took so long for me to answer your question about the Clarence Jordan Institute. This is a very hectic time of the year for us at best and we have been reconstructing our bookkeeping system which directly involves me.

LaDon's ideas are not mine. I said in the beginning that I had no objection to the idea and I still do not. I agree with you that a memorial does not have to be totally in accord with the one being memorialized. I feel that if the ideas that Clarence articulated are a basis for choosing the speakers and they can give the young men another view of what the ministry of the Word means and be an inspiration to them, this is good.

You and I know that Clarence was a unique person, called to things beyond that expected of most of us . . . able to see far beyond our vision. The fact that so many of the students came to me to say that Clarence had revolutionized their thinking made me feel comfortable with the idea of the institute. No two people are called to exactly the same task. I feel that many will hear and be aware of Clarence's life and teaching through this who otherwise might never have knowledge of his beliefs and discipleship.

Clarence did have definite ideas about money invested by Christian institutions in corporations that contribute to war and other destructive products. I think he expressed these freely when he last visited the seminary. LaDon had heard these ideas expressed many times.

I had looked forward to seeing you while you were in Florida and was disappointed that time did not allow you to come up and spend some time with us. Your visit would still be a welcome one.

Sincerely,
Florence Jordan

* * *

December 8, 1973

Dear Henlee:

I will be delighted to accept your gracious invitation to attend the first of the Clarence Jordan Institutes. David Graves had told me it was being planned for the spring and I had hoped to attend.

You will have to tell me a bit more about my responsibilities. What type of chapel talk, how formal, how long, what you had in mind, if you have a topic . . . you know the things I will have to be aware of. It will be good to be up there again.

Best wishes to you and your family in this Advent season.

Affectionately,
Florence Jordan
Mrs. C. L. Jordan

* * *

May 6, 1974

Dear Florence:

This is to say again how happy we were to have you on our campus for the Clarence Jordan Institute. Many faculty members and students have voluntarily expressed to me their genuine delight in having the opportunity to hear you in chapel and in the classrooms. One faculty member observed that you have "a lovely voice and that your joy comes through the words you speak."

At the present time we are discussing just how we can have another Clarence Jordan Institute next year. If you have any ideas, let us hear from you. As you know, we centered our first institute around the Bible because Clarence was a biblical scholar and translator. Perhaps next time we can center around the problem of race and then economics, etc.

I apologize for this small honorarium, but as you know we have a long way to go in our fund-raising campaign. Maybe we can tap some financial resources that will strengthen our budget.

Helen joins me in sending greetings and affection. It was a delight to have you in our home for dinner.

Gratefully,
Henlee Barnette

* * *

June 2, 1974

Dear Henlee:

Home at last with a little time to write letters. As usual, things were moving when I returned. Last weekend we had one of our seminars for ourselves. Brother Thomas from the Monastery of the Holy Ghost, at Conyers, Ga. was with us. Our discussion was on prayer. I thought it was rather good. I also had a house guest. This weekend we have had the board of directors meeting.

Finally, there is time to rethink some of the things that happened while I was away. I appreciate all the kindness shown me while I was on the campus. Please relay my thanks to Dale Moody, Paul Simmons, the McCalls, the Staggs, and any one else I may have overlooked. There were so many who were gracious and welcoming.

I needed no honorarium for the pleasure of speaking and being with all of you. Here is my check for $100 of it.

You asked me if I had any ideas about the institute. Your idea of changing it to a fall meeting sounded very good. I appreciated Bob Bratcher's willingness to come and speak, but with no reflection on Bob, I feel that the speakers should be persons who have a more radical

Christian message. In this time of social upheaval, we need to hear ideas of making the gospel more relevant to this world we live in. You know what I mean.

It was really good to be back in Louisville and see so many friends. Just wish I could have stayed a while longer. Wish you and Helen would have the chance to come down here.

Your friendship meant much to Clarence and to me, Henlee. I enjoyed the time I spent with you. Don't think you have changed a mite. I love your freedom . . . and you.

Florence

* * *

July 23, 1976

Dear Henlee:

The delay in answering your letter has been long. I have been away from the farm for a month.

I guess the easiest way is to take your questions in order. Yes, Hamilton Jordan is the son of Clarence's first cousin. His family lives in Albany and have been to Koinonia. Of course, these have been family visits, but Hamilton and his brother, did come up on their own and talk with us. I do not know where, or if, he attends church.

When asked about Jimmy Carter, I am at a loss. Although we live only seven miles from Plains, I am not acquainted with Mr. Carter. I think Clarence met him, but certainly the relationship was not one that mattered. Most of our business has been done in Americus and Albany, much larger trading centers. When we did business in Plains, it was usually with Mr. Williams. So far as I know, we have never done much, if any, business with Carter.

As to his ability, I know only what is in the newspapers . . . what they have written, past and present, which makes me no authority.

We are not a political group as you know. We do no block voting . . . each person votes according to personal preferences and feelings.

About a speaker. Do you know John Howard Yoder? He is a professor at one of the Mennonite seminaries. Just at the moment, I do not remember which.

Thanks for the note about Mr. Steilberg, I'll drop him a note.

I hope all goes well with you and yours these days. They are momentous days in our history and I am not without concern.

Affectionately,
Florence

* * *

May 18, 1977

Dear Henlee:

I just read your first note before the second one came. Arrived home last evening (17th) after a good visit with the children in Elkhart.

I truly enjoyed the stay at the seminary. It always amazes me that so many of the young people feel so close to Clarence, as though they had known him. His spirit does come through.

Millard said he had invited you to be on the Habitat board and I told him I'd asked if you'd consider a place on Koinonia's at our next vacancy. We both had the same thought.

Yes, I do have a Social Security number though I don't know why. I've never earned a penny under it. It is listed—Florence K. Jordan. . .

Did you and Helen have a good time on your speaking together? Of course you did, but I thought about you both.

Love,
Florence

* * *

Dear Henlee:

The check from the seminary has arrived and it was so generous that I felt able to give some of it to meet a need of a friend. Thanks!

Millard tells me that you have accepted his invitation to be on the board of directors of Habitat for Humanity. I am glad that you did accept. I hope now that you will be able to fill our next vacancy on the board for Koinonia Partners. When he told me he had invited you, I told him I had mentioned your serving with K.P.'s.

You know that we are not under the same charter. When Millard came home and told of his hopes for international housing, we did not feel that K.P. should include that work. We were afraid of spreading ourselves too thin. We will work together as much as possible and be vitally concerned for both projects. Habitat has set up offices in Americus. Until they have established their tax-exempt status, Koinonia will handle all money sent to them.

I am working on collecting some papers for the Jordan files at the seminary. When I have gone over a few more that may be duplicates, I'll send them on.

Affectionally,
Florence

* * *

June 2, 1977

Dear Florence:

Thanks for your good letter of May 31. It is always a pleasure to hear from you. I am glad that you received your small check for the great service which you rendered here at Southern Seminary when you spoke to our classes and dialogued with our students.

It would be a high honor to serve on the board of directors of Koinonia Partners. I shall look forward to that opportunity.

I am delighted that you are collecting some papers for the Jordan files at the Seminary. They will be carefully bound and placed in the library for future reference and research. You will be delighted to know that other professors here are beginning to devote sections in their courses to Clarence Jordan. A number of papers are being written in classes. I had hoped that one of my graduate students would do a doctoral dissertation on Clarence, but that will come later.

Helen joins me in sending love to you and all of our comrades in the faith at the Koinonia Partners.

I do hope that the young men who join the farm for the summer will do a commendable piece of work.

I believe that you are going to be swamped with visitors this summer and from now on since you are so close to Plains.

With warmest personal regards and affection, I remain

Gratefully,
Henlee Barnette

* * *

August 13, 1982

Dear Florence:

Thanks so much for the corrections on the two papers about Clarence. I have corrected each accordingly.

Enclosed find copies of letters I have received about Clarence. W.A. Criswell thought Clarence was "sort of to himself." This is incredible until you learn that all Criswell did at the seminary was, as one man said, "to keep his nose in books and preach on weekends."

I have requested that *** send me his biographical data and I will submit it to any church needing a pastor which I feel that he would be interested in.

Hope all goes well. Take care of yourself.

Affectionately,
Henlee Barnette

* * *

April 15, 1983

Dear Henlee:

Seeing you always adds to my pleasure in being in Louisville. Knowing you would be at the banquet, I had already planned to "hitch" a ride with you. I figured my brother could take me to Crescent Hill church, and I could have you take me back to his place.

You are one of the people who could write a good account of Clarence. Too many who did not really know him have tried to write and I feel have done a poor job.

I have been asked to make my "speech" on some anecdotes about Clarence that have not been published. You might want to think of one you heard or took part in.

I will probably fly into Louisville on Monday, the 18th. If George has to go to Ohio, I would arrive on Saturday, the 16th. I never mind a few days with family.

It will be good to see you all.

Florence

* * *

May 13, 1983

Dear Helen and Henlee:

As always, it was great to be with you. I am glad we were able to be together at least a little bit. Why don't you slow up a bit and come down Georgia way? I'd love to have you.

My one week away from Koinonia stretched into three as I visited with family in Louisville and then went on to Raleigh, N.C. for a visit with my sons. The visit to Raleigh was totally unplanned. I had said I was not going, but Lenny, who is with UPS came to Louisville to inspect their "Airlift"; the hub is at Staniford Field, and he persuaded me to fly on to Raleigh. A plane ticket and confirmed reservation sorta decided me.

I loved being with you both.

Florence

* * *

April 15, 1986

Dear Henlee and Helen:

I'm so glad that Paul had you come to supper with us. Coming to Louisville and not seeing you would be like coming home and not seeing the family. You have been such a dear friend for so long and Helen has just naturally become a part of that love.

Thanks for being what you are.

Love,
Florence

* * *

Appendix 2

Reflections by Some
Whose Lives Were Enriched
because They Knew Him

The following reflections are responses to a questionnaire. Most of the respondents were in seminary with Clarence or had come to know him later, some casually and some intimately. Each was requested to answer as many as possible of the following questions.

- How did you come to know him and how well did you know him?
- How did he impress you as a person?
- Relate what you know about his Koinonia group on the seminary campus. Name as many members as you can.
- Record any interesting incident in his life that you witnessed.
- To what extent did Clarence influence you in your own intellectual and spiritual pilgrimage?

Martin England
cofounder of Koinonia Farm

Clarence Jordan and I met at a meeting of the Louisville chapter of the Fellowship of Reconciliation in the spring of 1942. Clarence had read a letter I had written to Dr. Walt N. Johnson, of Mars Hill, North Carolina. Dr. Johnson had been executive secretary of the Baptist State Convention of Louisiana and of the Baptist State Convention of North

Carolina. Later, he became an executive in the Southern Baptist Seventy-Five Million Campaign. He had retired from all executive responsibility and settled in Mars Hill to study, to teach, and to inspire church leaders with a new commitment to stewardship. He issued a newsletter he called "The Next Step in the Churches." Both Clarence Jordan and I had followed Dr. Johnson's teachings with great interest, and both of us had been drawn to his unconventional views on what Christian stewardship meant. I had written a letter to Dr. Johnson in which I expressed the hope that a new community of believers might be gathered in which people of all races and classes might come together to work as equals, sharing a common purse as did the Christian community described in the Acts of the Apostles.

Clarence had read my letter to Dr. Johnson, and when we met, he immediately asked that we arrange to talk further on the topics I had begun to explore in my letter. From that time on, we met often. His wife Florence and my wife Mabel joined in the talks whenever possible.

It was at the England home in Wakefield, Kentucky, the four of us sat late into the night talking as, by this time, we often did. One (I believe it was Clarence) asked, "Well, what are we waiting for?" We had explored the idea of a Christian community in our talks, often and long. We had reached a common ground of understanding and agreement, and we pledged ourselves to undertake an experimental demonstration of a community modeled after the one described in the Book of Acts.

We decided that our experiment should be based on a farm. (Clarence had taken his undergraduate work in agriculture at the University of Georgia.) We also believed we would find a higher proportion of desperately poor people in Southeast Alabama and Southwest Georgia, areas with which Clarence had some acquaintance. We visited Tuskeegee Institute in Alabama, then went across into Sumter County, Georgia, where we found the tract of land which became Koinonia Farm.

* * *

H. Cornell Goerner
former area director (Africa)
of the Foreign Mission Board, SBC,
now Pastor of Elon Baptist Church, Ruther Glen, Virginia

Clarence Jordan was the most completely dedicated Christian I have ever known. With childlike simplicity he took the Sermon on the Mount seriously and tried to follow the teachings of Jesus literally and absolutely. His life was to me personally a rebuke and a challenge. It forced me to come to grips with the question, how far should one take the words of Jesus literally and idealistically, and at what point it is wiser to make adjustments to the practical realities of modern-day living. Obviously, I decided to rationalize and make practical adjustments, which I knew were, in the eyes of Clarence, "compromises." It left me a bit uncomfortable, but I could not go all the way with him—a course which would presumably have led to complete pacifism, nonresistance, and a sort of Christian communism, with the renunciation of private property, the profit motive, and the [free] enterprise system.

If there was any part of the Sermon on the Mount Clarence did not fully follow, I suppose it was the injunction "Judge not, that you be not judged" (Matthew 7:1). He seemed to be judgmental, and was at times a bit stern in condemning those who honestly could not agree with his own strict interpretation of the Scriptures. This came to a dramatic climax in one incident in which I was only indirectly involved.

It was sometime in 1941. I was a young assistant professor at Southern Seminary, and a member of the advisory committee of the Union Gospel Mission, a downtown mission project which had recently been turned over to the Long Run Baptist Association. Clarence had just completed his seminary work and received a Ph.D. in New Testament. He was made superintendent of city missions in Louisville, Kentucky, by the Association. A project somewhat similar to Union Gospel Mission was called "The Fellowship Center," housed in a large old residence. Several mission workers who received modest salaries were provided living quarters at the Fellowship Center as part of their support. I believe the residents of the Center at the time of the crisis were Clarence and Florence Jordan, Bob and Margaret Herndon, and perhaps Mr. and Mrs. Victor Glass.

Clarence had long wanted to live with a group which would seek to reproduce the early Christian community described in Acts 4:32: "All believers were one in heart and mind. No one claimed that any of his possessions was his won, but they shared everything they had" (NIV). Clarence apparently used his influence as association superintendent to persuade other workers to adopt this communal lifestyle. Bob and Margaret may have had reservations, but decided to try it.

All salaries were pooled. Meals were prepared jointly and served in a common dining room. Household bills were paid from the central fund from which each worker drew an allowance for his or her basic needs as determined by the group. Any exceptional expense must be submitted to the Fellowship, which must decide whether it was essential and allowable in view of other needs and the total resources of the group.

Things went smoothly for a while. Then it was discovered that Margaret was expecting a baby—her first. Medical bills had to be paid from the Fellowship funds, and it was understood that the normal fees would be provided. After all, Florence Jordan was also expectant. But at a certain point, Bob and Margaret become anxious about her condition and asked the Fellowship to authorize some special type of medical advice or therapy, which they felt was needed but was a bit expensive. The group considered the request, but decided that he procedure was optional and could be omitted without undue risk. The Fellowship refused to authorize the expense. Margaret was distressed and fearful. Bob manfully decided that his wife's health was at stake and that her life and that of the baby might be jeopardized. After a painful session, the couple withdrew from the Fellowship preferring to handle their own personal finances. Bob soon gave up his work with the association and entered the chaplaincy.

I never attended a meeting of the Fellowship, but Bob came to me for counsel and to explain his position. Utterly sincere, he deplored the breach of fellowship, but felt that he must give priority to his wife's welfare. He revealed that he had never been completely convinced of the workability of the plan but agreed to try it as an experiment. This unfortunate incident practically killed the original "Koinonia,"[1] but it did not discourage Clarence. Within a year he decided to transfer the experiment to a rural setting—his original purpose, I believe, from which the city missions project had been a temporary deviation. Joined by Martin England and his wife, he and Florence established the now well-known Koinonia Farm near Americus, Georgia. There conditions were more favorable, because of the simple rural lifestyle within which individual members must adjust to the group; but more radical, because of the presence of poorly educated black farmers who were admitted to the Fellowship surrounded by a hostile, race-prejudiced Georgia environment. But there they made the experiment work! It was, and is one of the boldest social experiments ever projected in the South, as well as a beautiful demonstration of Christian love in action!

I still think of Clarence Jordan as a starry-eyed idealist, at most out of touch with the real world in which we must live. I cannot quite see how his simplistic, naive New Testament principles can be applied to the total social and economic system. But I am glad he was willing to try it. And I can never quite get away from the gnawing suspicion that, if enough of us would agree to create and live consistently within a true New Testament Koinonia, we could make it work, and it would change the world!

* * *

---

[1]He refers perhaps to an original group on the seminary campus. I do not have any accurate information on the group Clarnence tried to form on campus. I believe I was invited to join, but could not see my way to do so. I had only vague indirect reports of how it fared, and do not recall names of members. But see the reflection by Bob Herndon, below.

James L. Sullivan
former executive secretary-treasurer
of the Southern Baptist Sunday School Board

Clarence and I were schoolmates at the Southern Baptist Theological Seminary. While we were friends and thought highly of each other, our paths seemed to part after seminary days and fellowships never got renewed. The separation came more because of geography than anything else. He pursued his interests in his part of the world, while I served diligently elsewhere. None of this was due to misunderstandings or our basic philosophical or theological differences.

Perhaps Victor Glass can give you more insight than anyone else. He started out with Clarence in his Georgia project, but saw that if his ministry was to have the impact for which he sought that he would have to operate from a broader base. Hence he went to the Home Mission Board (SBC) for a most effective ministry where his influence could be more profound and permanent.

Clarence was as "clean as a hound's tooth" morally. I never knew him to do a little or questionable thing.

Aside from the classroom where I recognized his brilliance and creativity, I knew him best in the "Josephus Bowl" and flying kites in the strong March winds. While Clarence seemed to be a quiet soul, he was basically very competitive. He seemed kind and gentle as a mother, but he tackled in football like a fierce tiger. He could be both fierce and enduring. He was one who never gave up and called it quits, however fierce the opposition might have been. That same persistence was displayed throughout his life.

When flying kites, he always had to have a different kind, and he tried to fly his higher than anyone else. In his creativity he tried many models, which he made himself. He was always trying to find a better way to do things. Again, his creativity and persistence showed through.

Another thing I noticed. He always had an eye for people who were different, and especially for those he considered unfortunate. He not only sided with them, but he sought to help them. If a great group of people were together he would have an eye for the ones who were not white, not Southern, not Baptist, and not American. His closest friendships seemed, even during seminary days, to be among these. The same course was followed throughout his life. It was his basic nature. Seemingly, God made him that way.

I cannot say that Clarence influenced me any more than my other friend, but his attitudes, high ethical standards, and tenderness did impress me positively. I somehow never had contact with his Koinonia movement, but was aware of it. Too, I sought to keep up with its ups and downs because of my admiration of him. My personal position and methodology more nearly paralleled that of Victor Glass, but I was always ready to defend Clarence and the route which he thought as the better way.

* * *

J. Winston Pierce
minister, counselor, lecturer

I cannot help you much about Clarence; he and I came to Louisville the same year. We were friendly but not close. I do remember that by the second year I along with every other single man, possibly some married ones too, were envious of him in dating the lovely creature who became his wife! I was at Louisville only two years, went on to the University of Chicago. Clarence, of course, stayed. In the years that followed, our paths would cross when we were on the same programs at Ridgecrest or Mercer, or Alabama, etc. I admired him from afar, was always stimulated and rebuked by his teaching and living. His writing was helpful also, especially his translating.

* * *

W. W. Finlater
retired pastor of Pullen Memorial Baptist Church
Raleigh, North Carolina

I went to school with Clarence and admired him very much. Though I ran into him often—he was one year ahead of me—I was unaware of his kind of commitment and thought that I had predicted the future that lay ahead of him. But I was also in school with the pastor of the First Baptist Church in Dallas, Texas, who, as I recall, was a graduate student and I had not predicted that he would follow Dr. George Truett and do what he has done in the years thereafter!

Clarence has influenced me mostly from a distance because our paths crossed so rarely. I have recognized in him a man of great courage and deep commitment. He was a man who was not out trying to look radical or inviting martyrdom. He simply became more and more convinced of what simple gospel living and simple gospel preaching are. That is what got him into trouble in Georgia. Actually, it would have gotten him into trouble anywhere which is what the authentic gospel is supposed to do.

(Incidentally, his son is living in Raleigh and came to speak two successive Sundays to one of our church school classes. He told us, in such a beautiful and unpretentious way, the kind of man his father was, and also the kind of woman his mother is.)

Clarence has been with me in spirit all of my ministry and I can never survey and compute what he has meant to me in that respect. He has been a continuing inspiration.

* * *

Dale Moody
senior professor of Theology
the Southern Baptist Theological Seminary

Soon after the [Ohio and Mississippi River valley] flood in [January-February] 1937, I hitchhiked into Louisville on a strawberry truck early one morning. As I came up from Grinstead Drive and went through Mullins Hall on the campus of Southern Baptist Seminary, I looked across toward Norton Hall and saw what looked like L'il Abner walking toward us. He was one of the most handsome young men I've ever seen. As we approached one another he stuck out his big hand and said, "I'm Clarence Jordan."

I told him that I was Dale Moody and I had just arrived on the campus. Immediately he asked me if I'd had anything to eat! Of course I had not, so he told me to come along with him to breakfast because Florence was cooking a good Georgia breakfast at that very moment. I did just that and soon found that Florence was just as gracious as Clarence. That was the beginning of my friendship with Clarence Jordan.

I soon discovered that Clarence was tutoring students in the Greek New Testament. In those days, students were required to read all of the Greek New Testament before they could graduate. Therefore, a lot of "parallel" reading was going on, and some of the students badly needed a tutor. Clarence asked me to attend one of the sessions. When he discovered that I could read the Greek New Testament, he soon turned the tutoring over to me. That I did for that summer and for the next two summers even though I began before I registered in a course. My love for the Greek New Testament strengthened my relationship with Clarence Jordan.

In 1948 I was on the campus of the University of California. One of the first things I was asked—when people learned that I was a Southern Baptist—was whether I knew Clarence Jordan or not. I was surprised and pleased to learn that he had taken the campus by storm. They spoke of this handsome man standing up before students with the Greek New Testament in his hand and expounding the Sermon on the Mount as if he thought everybody should realize that that was the way to live. Those that I spoke with looked upon him as one of the most authentic Christians they had ever met. They had some difficulty in seeing how so much genuine piety and scholarship should be packed into a person that looked like the comic strip L'il Abner. I suppose the best way to describe him is that he was a pious and scholarly L'il Abner.

Later on in life I was able to visit Koinonia Farm and see how he transformed the land with the help of others. Even while he was at the seminary he would preach at churches in Kentucky and Indiana and cull their newborn hens from roosters while he visited on their farms. More than once I have followed him in a church. They had great joy in telling how a good Bible preacher could improve the number of good laying hens on the farm!

In brief, I think of Clarence Jordan as a marvelous combination of the best piety in Baptist history and the finest scholarship in the Southern Baptist Theological Seminary. He made a great impression on my life as he did with so many others. It is a pleasant memory for me to write these brief words out of love and appreciation.

* * *

Bob Herndon
retired colonel, United States Army

In 1935 there was a Negro mission in Louisville on Madison Street which has now been torn down. It had marble steps, tile floors, and a large room with a fountain in the middle of it. This was once one of the most famous houses of prostitution in the city of Louisville. The fountain sprayed water and the girls would dance nude around it. There were two bathrooms and eight individual rooms assigned to each girl which we later used as Sunday School rooms. The books that the Madam kept on each girl would show how many customers, how many hamburgers she ate, how much beer she drank, how much money she took in, and how much money the house received as their cut. Each girl went by first name only. There was Mamie, Martha, Louise, Lucille, and Wilma, just to name a few.

On the steps going to the second floor where the bedrooms were located there was a devil's head carved in wood on the lower part of the banister, and on one of the wooden walls someone had carved, "House of Sin." This place was called under the new name "Sunshine Center." Later, it became "Fellowship Center."

The word Koinonia is a Greek word that has many meanings. Five come to my mind at the moment. They are living together, worshipping together, sharing together, studying together, and praying together. This can best be accomplished where all of the participants live together and work together, as was set up at the Koinonia Farm near Americus, Georgia, between Plains and Americus, Georgia. The group was first started by Clarence and myself with about twelve individuals or couples. I will try to name as many as I can remember: Furman Urley, Texas; Howard and Barbara McClain, Columbia, South Carolina; Mr. and Mrs. John McGinnis, Knoxville, Tennessee. These are all I can think of at the present time since it has been so long ago. To the best of my knowledge, the group that started at the Southern Baptist Theological Seminary in Louisville, Kentucky, does not exist today. We all had such small incomes. As in my case, my wife and I had but $100 to put in and it took the whole $100 for us to live so we withdrew the full amount. Thus we were not able to share with the others in this way. [This campus group] was based on some of the same principles as the Koinonia Farm in Americus, Georgia.

Clarence Jordan was a native of Talbotton, Georgia, in Talbot County near Columbus. He attended the University of Georgia and received a B.S. degree in Agriculture and possibly a Masters degree in Agronomy. He was a brilliant student, a scholar, a dynamic Christian who truly believed in the brotherhood of man. His wife, Florence, whom he married at the seminary, was a brilliant and thoroughly Christian lady. They were unselfish, loved their fellow man and cared for others' needs and, since our little mission was in a predominately Negro neighborhood, we catered mainly to blacks. Most of the teachers were from the Baptist Training School and the seminary. This was the beginning of an active Negro program in the Southern Baptist Convention. We worked together about two or three years before the beginning of a great idea of Christian service and cooperation and living among our black brothers.

Clarence and Florence had wonderful personalities. Clarence was a Greek shcolar as well as of the English New Testament. He was one of the finest people I ever knew. His background was Southern (Georgia). But the thing that made him and most of the people in the Koinonia different was their Christian philosophy and acceptance of Christ. *That* made the difference.

Clarence and I remained friends until his death. We came to know each other and I think we knew each other very well on race issues. Clarence was brilliant, humble, had a great personality, and had a great love for his fellow man. Before becoming director of the Fellowship Center, he served a little church about thirty miles from Louisville among some of the poorest people in rural Kentucky. Clarence and Florence had hearts and personalities and a love that embraced all people of all races, colors and creeds. I was privileged to have known them both.

It was my idea that those of us who couldn't make a contribution as an agronomist could make other contributions through canning, curing of hams and meats, packaging peanuts and pecans, leather work, wood work, making of candies, metal work, sewing, and thus selling these to make possibly enough money to help with the farming and raising of cattle, hogs, chickens, etc. We all differed slightly in our opinions on how the Koinonia should function but there was never a misunderstanding among any of the group to my knowledge. Clarence was a pacifist and wanted nothing to do with the military. I, too, was opposed to war as I am today but I went about it in a different manner. My wife and I have always worked against causes of war such as poverty, brutality, hunger, illiteracy, prejudices and all of the things that cause men to fight each other. We differed on this approach. After Clarence left the Fellowship Center, I succeeded him along with a Negro as cosuperintendent. We worked together in harmony until I went into the chaplaincy in early 1942. His name was Cecil Torrence, a very fine man. When I left he remained on as superintendent.

Some of the young men and women who worked with us at the Sunday School Center and Fellowship Center still speak of this as one of the greatest experiences in their lives. They were helpful, studious, loving, and kind and continually giving of themselves among the black youth of Madison Street and the southwest section of Louisville.

. . . If I could describe Clarence, I would say that he truly was a "Saint in overalls." He knew farming, he followed the teachings of Jesus. His wife Florence was a great insipiration and help in every way possible—a great lady. Their neighbors and friends were Jimmy and Rosalyn Carter and their family. We spent many hours trying to put the Koinonia together that it might work for the good of all.

I think one reason Koinonia was not as successful on the campus was because we did not live together, worship together, share together, study together, pray together, and eat together. We tried to do this but due to necessity we had to go our separate ways. When it is practiced on a farm or in a condominium, it works better.

* * *

Frank Stagg
senior professor of New Testament Interpretation
the Southern Baptist Theological Seminary

Thank you for the opportunity to join the friends of Clarence Jordan in recalling what we remember of him and in tribute to him. Our acquaintance began in the academic year 1932–1933, and our friendship grew until his untimely death.

I first met Clarence in Nashville, at a meeting of state Baptist Student Union presidents, he from Georgia and I from Louisiana. Through this relationship, I saw him again at [the Baptist assembly at] Ridgecrest, North Carolina. It may surprise many, but my first impression of Clarence was as a humorist and entertainer. He reenacted for us the famous midnight ride of Paul Revere, making rider and horse come alive, with beating hooves, flapping garments, the shouted warnings, and the whole bag. Some may have known him only as an agitator and man of conflict, but I first knew him as a gentle person with warmth and a sense of humor. But in those early encounters with Clarence through B.S.U., I also saw another dimension in him, that would take him ever deeper into a crusade for human rights and thus into conflict. Clarence had an enlightened conscience, alertness to what was going on around him, keen insight into the intention of Jesus, and courage even as a college student to make existential what he increasingly found exegetically in the Greek New Testament.

It was during our college days through B.S.U. that I first heard Clarence speak out on current issues. My memory is that it was against war that I first heard him speak out, and later against racial injustice. Clarence told us about his moment of truth as he was engaged in military practice in a cavalry unit. He was supposed to charge on horseback, running his spear through a human dummy. It was then that he realized that he could not kill another human being, even as a soldier in war. What he first had to struggle through for himself became nonnegotiably essential to the witness which by conscience and conviction he was compelled to give wherever he had a hearing.

As I remember it, I next heard Clarence express views on race relations new to me. I believe Clarence Jordan was the first Christian I ever heard explicitly challenge war and discrimination against black people. These were issues with which I had to struggle, and it was with pain at every step. I do not know what inner struggles Clarence may have had at the outset, except as indicated above. Since his early environment closely paralleled mine, I assume that the road was not easy.

Clarence and I should have been classmates at Southern Seminary, but I fell behind him by taking a year out between high school and college to find vocational direction and a year out between college and seminary to prepare for both marriage and seminary. Although not classmates in seminary, our years at Southern did overlap; and it was in graduate work that we were closest. We both majored in Greek New Testament. Clarence loved the Greek New Testament and mastered it, both as to its language and intention. One requirement of us was that we run every reference in A. T. Robertson's "big grammar," through all 1,454 pages with a dozen or more citations on most pages. Clarence acknowledged to me that much of this was "dishwashing," jumping here and there, back and forth, all over the Greek New Testament; but he said that the joy of it was that it kept your nose right in the Greek New Testament all the time. Clarence found more than forms and syntax; he found the example and teaching of Jesus.

The rest of the story while Clarence was in Southern Seminary can be told better by others, and his life and work after seminary days are known far and wide. I cherished Clarence as a friend and found a better sense of direction and some measure of courage for a ministry which seeks to be both biblically based and currently relevant. Thank you, Clarence!

* * *

C. Conrad Browne
pastor, First Baptist Church, Iowa City, Iowa

During the year before the end of World War II, Clarence Jordan was an evangelist at Calvary Baptist Church in Washington, D.C. One of my friends told me about the unusual messages of this deep South farmer-preacher-translator. The Word took on flesh through the abilities of this man's preaching. His readings from the Greek New Testament brought a clarity unlike I had ever before experienced. *Koinonia*, a word which I did not know how to spell, was his great theme. *Koinonia,* a word I was slow to pronounce, became a burning fire, an unquenchable thirst which developed into such a passion that toward the end of divinity school one professor was to remark, "Can't you talk, or write, about anything else?"

The military draft kept me, at that time, from tracking Clarence Jordan to south Georgia. By the time I was free from selective service, the call to go on to theological education had taken precedence over immediate involvement in Koinonia. The idea boiled and roiled on a back burner.

During the summer of 1949, the University of Chicago Divinity School asked me to represent it at a young people's conference at Greek Lake Baptist Assembly. Clarence Jordan was the Bible study leader. We talked, and as I learned, a great yearning came upon me to be a part of that way of life. Several of us in that gathering covenanted to make the journey to Georgia and investigate the excitement Clarence had fired in us.

In August that year, Mrs. Browne and I experienced the South for the first time. It was to be November before we finished school and earned enough money to buy passage and move to Americus, Georgia. We stayed for nearly fourteen years (until 1963). Clarence remarked many times that of all the potential participants, we seemed the least likely to make the grade in a farm community.

* * *

Victor Glass

I first learned about Clarence Jordan from a college classmate of mine who went to the seminary a year ahead of me. We both graduated together from Carson-Newman College, but I took a year at Vanderbilt to do some study there and he went on to the seminary. And in the course of that year and the following summer he talked to me about Clarence and about what he was doing in Louisville and this influenced my decision to come to Louisville and enroll in seminary. Clarence first gave Edith and me a place to live, on the top floor of Union Gospel Mission. We worked there on a part-time basis. I did some boys work and worked with the scouts and did a little janitorial service and argued with Miss Brewster from time-to-time, and Edith got to know Clarence pretty well since she accompanied him a lot in his singing. (He did enjoy singing as well as preaching.)

Clarence impressed me as being a man in the tradition of the apostle Paul. He was a man who had scholarship and integrity, and the energy and desire for work to put into practice what he learned from his mind into his muscles and into his hands and into his feet. Clarence used to tell a story, how at the seminary they would always say to him, "Well, Clarence, you know you're right theologically and exegetically, you know you're right, but . . . ," and that was always the only excuse for not trying to do some of the things Clarence wanted to do. He also impressed me as being able to do the hard work on the field and relate to all kinds of people, but he could also impress the intelligentsia and get to the pocketbooks of people who had money even though they were not willing to invest their time and effort and personalities in working in some areas where there might be conflict. He got very good agency support when he got ready to leave Louisville and go to his farm at Koinonia; that certain presence in Louisville helped him to be able to do this. So all in all, Clarence helped me to see that you needed scholarship—and I wish I had more of it—but he also impressed on me that if scholarship and research could not be put into the hard cold facts of life, it wasn't very good. There was a wide gap during seminary days—as there continues to be among Christian people—between what we know to be and what is clear and we do not follow the full leadership of the spirit in putting it into person. All in all, I hold up Clarence as one of the fine persons who came into my life early as a young theologue and helped me to find some good directions for my own life.

Clarence was a great one for interpreting life by taking it down to the real bare facts and putting the Scriptures to it and giving substance to it. One night he was preaching at Union Gospel Mission. He was preaching on the bread of life and the word becoming flesh, and he had in the pulpit there with him a piece of loaf bread (just a slice of it) and Clarence was looking at it and explaining all about it as he was so well able to do. He was an agriculture major in college and I'm sure that's what helped influence him in the Koinonia Farm experiment. He could make a living out of dirt, besides relating that to his scholarship entries. Well, as Clarence talked about this bread and broke it down and explained it, and as he sort of got through with it, he just casually tossed the bread over onto the mantel piece in that old residence that housed Union Gospel Mission. He let it fly through the air and land over there and then he went on with his sermon. So he was a person who was sort of down to life, humble, folksy, but his brilliance often shone through. I think that is what challenged a lot of the seminary boys. And the black Baptists in Louisville were also in his corner and were able to accept him and to receive these white students in the various churches.

Clarence was the subject of one thing that I hear about. I'm not sure who told me about it or how true it is, and it's just something that I've heard and wouldn't want it to be used as known fact. It was said that, when Clarence was superintendent of missions in the Long Run Baptist Association, this young black man came into his office one day, very bitter and wanting to vent his anger on certain white people for what they were doing to blacks. He couldn't find any way to justify his feelings and anger except to put it into flesh and to flesh it out in his own life as a witness. As the story goes, Clarence went over in the corner and picked up something—I don't know what—and handed it to the young man, and then got down on his knees and put his head down and asked the young man, "Well, here I am, I'm white, you're black, take out your anger on me. Let this be an expression of your feeling if you want to do this, if you feel justified in doing it, if this will help you, go ahead and do it." I don't know if it has much truth to it or not, but it is a very good story.

I regarded Clarence as an intellectual giant, a man who was able to see through all the camouflage and able to ferret out in his own mind what the truth was and cut right to it, without so much building it up and watering it down until it didn't have much influence. That was an influence in my own life in terms of me furthering my studies for a doctorate myself. I felt a great need to balance intellect and spirituality with the actual hard and dirty work of putting them into practice. Clarence helped me to see that the intellectual part of a person and the spiritual part of him are one and the same and must be bonded and welded together in a united front, that to have the holy Joe attitude without the intellect and the knowledge was to go off the deep end. But also to have the intellectual capacity to know right and to be powerful in the mind and in the knowledge of seeing what was right and then not having the humility in spiritual power to balance it off . . . then the two really cut under each other and you end up nowhere fast, either emphasizing one or the other to the utter end and not putting them together. So Clarence helped me to see this as a young theologian and to help me to understand where was a good place to put my life. And I think maybe that I didn't know this until later, that you had to offer yourself to Koinonia. I thought maybe you had to be invited to go there, but I learned later that you went and sort of presented your own self. But I felt that at that point for me education and development and planting my life in the context of school was the right way to go and that's the way I followed. And I think to some degree this is what my pilgrimage was even at the Home Mission Board, to try to make an impact and I always felt and still do feel that the real problem in race in this country has never been black, because the overwhelming majority of the population has been white and the vote and the economic power and to some extent the cultural power helped determine where we're going to go as a spirit and I hope this will have some effect later on.

* * *